CAPSTONE REFE

THE
ULTIMATE BOOK
OF BUSINESS
SKILLS

CAPSTONE REFERENCE

Capstone Reference is the home of definitive resource books for the modern professional. Joining forces with Capstone's best-selling ***Ultimates***, all titles in the series are up to date, relevant, robust, comprehensive, accessible and – unlike so many other reference titles in the business section today – affordable!

The Capstone Encyclopaedia of Business	1-84112-053-7	£20
The Complete Small Business Guide	1-84112-079-0	£14.99
Business FAQs	1-84112-012-X	£16.99
The Ultimate Business Library	1-84112-059-6	£15.99
The Ultimate Book of Business Thinking	1-84112-440-0	£15.99
The Ultimate Business Guru Book	1-84112-075-8	£15.99
The Ultimate Book of Business Brands	1-84112-439-7	£15.99
The Ultimate Strategy Library	1-84112-180-0	£15.99

CAPSTONE REFERENCE

THE
ULTIMATE BOOK
OF BUSINESS
SKILLS

THE 100 MOST IMPORTANT TECHNIQUES FOR BEING SUCCESSFUL IN BUSINESS

TONY **GRUNDY** • LAURA **BROWN**

CAPSTONE

First published 2004 by
Capstone Publishing Limited (A Wiley Company)
The Atrium
Southern Gate
Chichester
West Sussex PO19 8SQ
http://www.wileyeurope.com

CIP catalogue records for this book are available from the British Library and the US Library of Congress

ISBN 1-84112-547-4

Typeset in Plantin by Sparks Computer Solutions Ltd
http://www.sparks.co.uk

Printed and bound by TJ International Ltd, Padstow, Cornwall

CONTENTS

10 Self-management Skills   261

11 Some Case Studies Linked to the 100 Business Skills   293

12 Conclusion   301

Introduction

1

WHAT IS THE ESSENCE OF MANAGEMENT?

Management is defined in the *Oxford English Dictionary* as: 'The process of an instance of managing or being managed', or 'The professional administration of business concerns'.

This implies that 'management' encompasses managing both self and others, and also that there is a process for doing it.

But a 'process' implies knowledge of, and ability to use, a range of business skills. And taking it as a given that you are, or wish to become, a manager, then our promise, as in that of the famous book the *Kama Sutra*, is that: 'There are a hundred different ways (at least) of doing it.'

So, in this 'Kama Sutra' of business skills we will take you through a hundred different types of business skills. Each one of these skills is carefully defined, explained, and is also linked to key techniques and contains tips on how to practise this particular skill.

Whilst many of these business skills can be practised independently, many also can be brought together in combination. It is rare in a complex management situation to be practising only one business skill at a time, so we have clustered these one hundred skills into nine categories as follows:

1   Strategy skills.
2   Marketing skills.
3   Commercial management skills.
4   Finance skills.
5   Operations skills.
6   Leadership skills.
7   Organizational skills.
8   Problem-solving skills.
9   Self-management skills.

In effect, we have also created a very useful framework for diagnosing management competencies – but this is essentially a spin-off benefit. Our main mission is to help you become more aware of which business skills you should be using – and when – in order that you build on these, and perform even better. Essentially, these skills are exactly those that we would, for example, look for in an MBA student who has bedded in his/her learning with some stretching, general management experience. These skills are now explored in our next section on self-diagnosis.

Business skills: self-diagnosis

This section exploits our framework of business skills by allowing you to perform a self-diagnosis of your skills profile – hopefully helping you to diagnose your key gaps.

We would like you to score yourself on each of the 100 skills using the following ratings:

5 = very strong indeed
4 = strong
3 = moderately strong
2 = not so strong
1 = weak

Strategy

Strategy skills span different forms of strategic decisions, including acquisitions, alliances and investment, and also general awareness of competitors and the global and economic environments. Strategy skills also entail helicopter thinking, storytelling, and risk and uncertainty analysis.

The hallmark of strategy skills is that they deal with particularly complex and often ambiguous factors – and require iterative and holistic thinking about the issues.

Strategy skills	5	4	3	2	1
Acquisitions appraisal					
Acquisitions and deal-making					
Alliances					
Competitor awareness					
Divestment					
Economic awareness (macro)					
Economic awareness (micro)					
Global awareness					
Helicopter thinking					
Regulatory awareness					
Risk and uncertainty analysis					
Storytelling					
Strategic thinking					

Marketing

Marketing begins with the customer and market awareness and then moves on into the phases of developing a marketing strategy (for example market segmentation, market research, market and product development, selling, and life-cycle management).

Marketing skills have a very close relationship with strategy skills.

Marketing skills	5	4	3	2	1
Brand management					
Customer awareness					
Life-cycle management					
Market awareness					
Market development					
Market research					
Market segmentation					
Product development					
Selling					

Commercial management

Commercial management covers contract management and it also covers targeting goals, margin management and contract management. Business cases, project appraisal and business planning are all infrastructure processes that need to be mastered. Commercial management has particularly close links with financial skills and strategic skills.

Commercial management	5	4	3	2	1
Business cases					
Business planning					
Contract management					
Margin management					
Negotiation					
Performance analysis					
Project appraisal					
Targeting goals					
Tendering					

Operations

Operations skills are highly diverse, focusing on projects, processes, technology/IT, resource management/re-engineering. They also include benchmarking as a process skill. Acquisition integration inevitably requires a multitude of these skills.

Operations skills	5	4	3	2	1
Acquisition integration					
Benchmarking					
Buying					
Controlling					
Information collection					
IT awareness					
Outsourcing					
Process management					
Project management					
Re-engineering					
Resource management					
Technology awareness					

Finance

Finance entails analytical skills (financial awareness, understanding company accounts, forecasting and budgeting) through to process skills like financial planning, cost management and value management. In addition at a commercial level we consider cash-flow management, and linked to strategy skills, we have turnaround.

Finance skills	5	4	3	2	1
Budgeting					
Cash-flow management					
Cost management					
Credit control					
Financial awareness					
Financial planning					
Forecasting					
Turnaround					
Understanding company accounts					
Value management					

Leadership

Leadership takes us into the softer skills areas – interspersed skills such as listening, empathizing and energizing through to process skills like chairing, change management and coaching.

Leadership skills also have a close relationship with strategy skills.

Leadership skills	5	4	3	2	1
Chairing					
Change management					
Coaching					
Direction setting					
Empathizing					
Energizing					
Facilitation					
Listening					
Motivating					
Policy setting					
Political awareness					
Stakeholder management					
Summarizing					

Organizational skills

Organizational skills extend the softer, interpersonal competencies into the cross-cultural arena, including delegating, influencing, interviewing, networking and teamworking. We also see some more process-based skills here like organizational design, organizational and people planning, performance appraisal and recruiting and training.

Report writing is another important skill to be developed.

Organizational skills	5	4	3	2	1
Cross-cultural skills					
Delegation					
Influencing					
Interviewing					
Networking					
Organizational design					
Organization and people planning					
Performance appraisal					
Recruiting					
Report writing					
Teamworking					
Training					

Problem-solving

Problem-solving requires a range of mental capacities including 'alien thinking', brainstorming, creativity, imagination, and the ability to deal with challenges. Option generation (which is clearly linked with the strategy skills) plays a critical role too.

Problem-solving	5	4	3	2	1
Alien thinking					
Brainstorming					
Building					
Challenging					
Creativity					
Imagination					
Option generation					
Problem diagnosis					
Questioning					

Self-management

Self-management covers a diversity of skills, from managing your drive, energy management and learning, through to managing issues (like prioritization). Stress and time management are also imperative in order to be fully effective.

Self-management	5	4	3	2	1
Action planning					
Being interviewed					
E-mail management					
Energy management					
Drive					
Learning					
Presentations (making them)					
Prioritization					
Proactivity					
Self-awareness					
Self-development					
Stress management					
Time management					

Now, add up your scores:

Skill set	Score
Strategy	
Marketing	
Commercial management	
Operations	
Finance	
Leadership	
Organizational skills	
Problem-solving	
Self-management	
Total score	

NB: if you would like to work out your score by each category, divide each score by the following quotient, and then multiply by 20, to get a percentage figure.

- Strategy ÷ 13
- Marketing ÷ 9
- Commercial management ÷ 9
- Operations ÷ 12
- Finance ÷ 10
- Leadership ÷ 13
- Organizational skills ÷ 12
- Problem-solving ÷ 9
- Self-management ÷ 13

So, how did you fare? Which areas could you improve in? What was your overall score, and to what extent was it focused on 'very strong'/'strong' in some areas, but not on others? If the score was uneven then it is quite possible that you might benefit from an MBA/or general one-year programme. If you feel you are being biased or subjective, re-read the relevant sections to get a more objective rating.

Each one of the above business skills is complex in its own right, and demands, as the *Oxford English Dictionary* implies, doing so professionally. But for the average manager, it may be hard to be proficient in each and every one of these hundred business skills. For instance, our very first one, 'Acquisitions Appraisal', demands the ability to analyse a company's strengths and weaknesses, *and* opportunities and threats from the outside, *and* from a multitude of perspectives. *The Ultimate Book of Business Skills* gives you both an overview of these 100 business skills, and a more in-depth analysis of each one. This is accomplished within the following format:

- definition of the skill,
- its pros and cons (where appropriate),
- when it is needed,
- the relevant techniques,
- killer takeaways, and
- links to other skills.

Strategy Skills

In this section, there is some variation in how complex these skills are, and also in the extent to which specific techniques exist for executing them. Also, in some cases we have illustrated the skills with real-world cases. So we will spend a little more time and space on some themes than on others, ensuring at the same time that we give good coverage and depth to each one.

ACQUISITIONS APPRAISAL

n acquisition is defined as: 'The purchase of a company or of part, or all of its net assets, either as part of your own strategy development, as a short/medium term vehicle for making a trading profit.'

'Acquisition appraisal' is now defined as: 'The process of understanding the value of a potential acquisition, involving a detailed analysis and evaluation of its current position and its prospects.'

The acquisition appraisal process is complex, involving the integration of not only the strategic perspective, but also of:

- marketing,
- finance,
- operations,
- IT,
- purchasing,
- organization and management, and
- legal and tax.

This range of skills is an unusual combination to have in just one person and, typically, acquisition appraisal requires an acquisition appraisal team (sometimes called an 'A-team'). This can be resourced either fully from a particular business unit, or by a combination of corporate/divisional and business unit staff. In unusual cases it is carried out principally by corporate/divisional management, but this has severe limitations, particularly because there is unlikely to be the same commitment (from within the business unit) for it to work.

As a process, acquisition appraisal is a 'must do' prior to buying a business – it is a disaster if the process is not handled thoroughly, professionally, and in appropriate depth.

There are, however, some pros and cons of acquisition generally, which it is useful to mention now.

The pros:

- acquisitions can speed up strategy development,
- they can be a means of making an increased profit,
- they are exciting challenges – at many levels, and
- they can possibly help develop the careers of your managers, and at the same time improving their financial rewards.

The cons:

- acquisitions are fraught with risk and uncertainty,
- on average, they destroy, rather than create shareholder value,
- they demand far more time (usually), than you thought,
- they involve integration which may be painful, and
- they can prove to be career-limiting.

Acquisition appraisal is needed whenever you are beginning to think about making an acquisition. To achieve it effectively, you will need to go through the following key stages:

- Defining your wider business objectives and strategy.
- Evaluating different routes to strategy development (and their pros and cons), including organic development, alliance, divestment and, of course, acquisitions.
- Identifying possible acquisition targets.
- Initial screening of these targets.
- Detailed evaluation of them, in terms of:
  - competitive strength,
  - future potential,
  - integration needs,
  - development needs,
  - financial attractiveness, and
  - appropriate funding strategy.

One of the most powerful techniques for integrating the acquisition appraisal is to deploy the strategic option grid (see key skill 'Option Generation', p.249), which spells out five key criteria, namely:

- strategic attractiveness,
- financial attractiveness,
- implementation difficulty,

- uncertainty and risk, and
- stakeholder acceptability.

This should be supplemented by more specific acquisition criteria – including some key must-haves and mustn't-haves.

A must-have might include, for example, acquiring a strong brand or a strong management team. A mustn't-have might include a 'lack of real cultural fit'.

Killer takeaways are:

- Understand the deal from the seller's perspective: have the 'out-of-body experience' – imagine being them.
- Establish a 'walk-away-from' price and stick with it.
- Don't get carried away with the 'thrill of the chase'.

Our key links to other skills are:

- acquisitions and deal-making (p. 18),
- acquisitions integration (p. 107),
- business cases (p. 79),
- divestment (p. 28),
- option generation (p. 249), and
- turnaround (p. 158).

References

Grundy, Tony (2003) *Smart Things to Know about Mergers and Acquisitions*, Capstone, Oxford.

Haspeslagh, P.C. & Jemison, D.B., (1991) *Managing Acquisitions*, The Free Press/Macmillan, New York.

ACQUISITIONS AND DEAL-MAKING

O ur definition of acquisition deal-making is: 'The process of managing the acquisition deal to secure financial advantage.'

The skill of acquisition deal-making is a unique one. One of the authors remembers his first exposure to acquisition deal-making many years ago in a senior management role in ICI, within its seeds business. He was a member of the A-team, who were responsible for developing the seeds business strategy via acquisition.

ICI had already made a number of major acquisitions of seeds businesses that, up and until that point, had not been particularly successful, even troublesome. But the division was (then) committed to expansion through acquisition, and there was a perceived need to pursue its acquisition programme as a pressing priority.

An opportunity then came up to acquire a seeds business that a conglomerate business had bought as part of a division of technology businesses. Incredibly, the conglomerate business actually had a major car manufacturing operation at its core. But the vendor saw no real reason why they should continue to hold a seeds business within their overall portfolio.

So they decided that a clever plan was to dispose of this seeds business to an agrochemicals business that was very keen to invest in seeds. This was to be a part of ICI's publicly known, diversification programme to shift outside its core business.

Unfortunately, however, it would appear that ICI were even more motivated to buy the business than the vendor was to sell. Matters came to a head when the ICI A-team met the opposition at a hotel near Charles de Gaulle airport, Paris. Regrettably, the ICI team exhibited signs of over-motivation in its pursuit of a deal. It proved difficult to drive a hard bargain as the vendor perceived the situation as being very much in their favour.

Some years later, the author met up with one of the vendor's advisers – actually at a Christmas party. She said: 'Oh ICI, we really screwed you, we really took you to the cleaners,' almost provoking an argument between two people whose relationship had previously been cordial.

This experience underlines the importance of managing the acquisition deal-making process as objectively as possible.

A most useful technique for helping think through this process is captured in Fig. 2.1. It shows the five deal-making forces that are likely to shape the eventual deal. They are:

- the range of options facing the acquirer,
- the range of options facing the vendor,
- the rivalry for a deal (with other potential bidders),
- the time pressure to do a deal – on the acquirer, and
- the time pressure to do a deal – on the vendor.

Some killer takeaways on deal-making include:

- Know your 'tradeables' in advance of the negotiation.
- Get early agreement on the essentials.
- Have a negotiation game plan in advance
- Keep an ongoing track of the value which you hope to gain from the deal (and of its potential costs).
- When negotiations get stuck, take time out and go back to the essentials/tradeables.
- Be absolutely clear who has the final say.

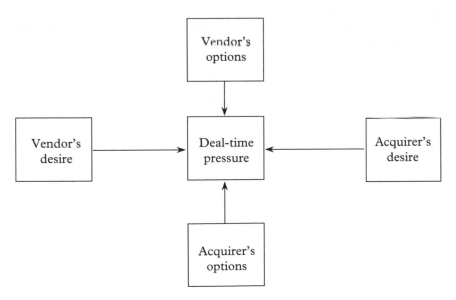

Fig. 2.1 Acquisitions – the five forces

The key links to other skills include:

- action planning (p. 263),
- business cases (p. 79),
- chairing (p. 171),
- contract management (p. 86),
- drive (p. 266),
- financial planning (p. 154),
- negotiating (p. 92),
- option generation (p. 249),
- self-awareness (p. 285),
- stakeholder management (p. 199),
- stress management (p. 289),
- storytelling (p. 47), and
- value management (p. 165).

Interestingly, this is quite a complex range of skills, spanning the analytical, the interpersonal and the political. This highlights how unusually difficult acquisition deal-making is, as an example of key business skill.

References

Grundy, Tony (2003) *Smart Things to Know about Mergers and Acquisitions*, Capstone, Oxford.

Haspeslagh, P.C. & Jemison, D.B. (1991) *Managing Acquisitions*, The Free Press/Macmillan, New York.

ALLIANCES

 n alliance can be defined as: 'A longer-term collaborative arrangement between two or more companies whose aim is to add more value to all parties than would be possible if they were to compete separately.'

Alliances vary in their time-horizons, in their scope, and in their structure. A strategic alliance typically entails not only a major longer-term commitment but also the pooling of resource to achieve common strategic goals. This may even take the form of setting up a separate legal entity with its dedicated resources.

The pros of alliances (and joint ventures) are:

- giving you access to markets which otherwise would be difficult or impossible,
- sharing and reduction of costs (e.g. R&D, distribution),
- pre-empting alliance opportunities that competitors would otherwise be able to exploit,
- enabling the company to compete against bigger players,
- developing existing competencies – or acquiring new ones, and
- opening up new opportunities and enabling existing constraints to be surmounted.

The cons of an alliance are:

- the investment – in shared assets (or own assets),
- the management effort, energy and time,
- the other potential alliances foregone, and
- developing organically (or by acquisition) – again the opportunities foregone.

While we have earlier assumed that alliances *minimize* investment, considerable resources are often needed to make an alliance effective (unless it is very loose and fluid). These are often underestimated by one or more of the alliance partners, resulting in subsequent disaffection.

In addition, alliances contain further downsides:

- the other alliance partner(s) emerges as dominant,
- the erosion, and ultimately loss, of own core competencies,
- overprotection of one's competencies (or by collaborators) makes it difficult (or impossible) to generate real synergies (Faulkner 1995),
- medium-term success is achieved – but then in the longer term the alliance breaks down because of unforeseeable reasons, and
- culture clash/mismatched expectations between partners.

In conclusion, strategic alliances thus appear to be relatively difficult to manage (Fig. 2.2).

A technique for understanding alliances is that, firstly, they might be the product of a 'deliberate' strategy (Mintzberg 1994) – that is, one which has been targeted and thought through against its external and internal context; longer as well as shorter term. A 'deliberate strategy' is one that comes from reflective, strategic thought, rather than through an opportunity merely popping up.

An emergent strategy is one that happens either by accident or by skilful positioning. An opportunity arises (or is created) by a meeting or by networking, and this gives rise to a collaborative arrangement.

As the alliance forms there is incoming investment of time, resources and commitment by the various alliance partners. As the alliance becomes operational, inevitably it evolves in interaction with the market and with

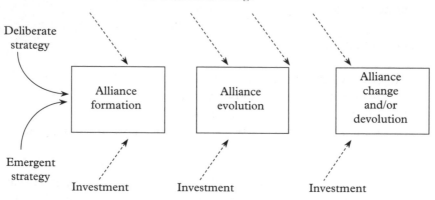

Fig. 2.2 Alliances dynamics

competitive forces and change. New strategic decisions are made (often incrementally, rather than as a systematic pattern), resulting in further evolution of the alliance.

Ultimately, the alliance may devolve (or dissolve) – its *raison d'être* having changed or disappeared.

Over the alliance's lifetime there are changing patterns of investment and of returns. The financial payback of the alliance has a profound impact on its evolution.

Killer takeaways associated with alliances are:

- Learn from your partner's new competencies.
- Be sensitive to cultural differences and cultural fit.
- Be 'transparent' to permit knowledge transfer.
- Have complementary assets and competencies – for a strategic fit.
- Ensure there is mutual support and trust.
- Start with a strong need to collaborate.
- Get the set-up arrangements for the alliance right (including provision for divorce).

Key links to other skills are:

- change management (p. 173),
- contract management (p. 86),
- cross-cultural skills (p. 207),
- direction setting (p. 179),
- financial planning (p. 154),
- global awareness (p. 38),
- influencing (p. 211),
- life-cycle management (p. 60),
- learning (p. 271),
- negotiating (p. 92),
- organizational design (p. 218),
- risk and uncertainty analysis (p. 44), and
- strategic thinking (p. 49).

References

Faulkner, D. (1995) *International Strategic Alliances*, McGraw Hill, Maidenhead.

Mintzberg, H. (1994) *The Rise and Fall of Strategic Planning*, Prentice Hall, Hemel Hempstead.

COMPETITOR AWARENESS

C | ompetitor awareness can be defined as: 'The activity of tracking a competitor's strategy, tactics and capability in order to attack them, to defend against them, or to learn from them.'

The pros of competitor awareness are:

- it alerts you to industry change, and may help trigger a review of your strategy,
- it might produce insights about how you can achieve increases in market share – at the expense of competitors, and
- it helps you to avoid having too internal a perspective on how you manage.

A possible con of competitor awareness is that it makes you more frightened of your competitors and thus more 'frozen' in your mindset.

Competitor awareness is needed particularly when:

- entering a new market, or developing a new product,
- there are major regulatory or technological changes impacting on the industry,
- customers are particularly demanding, and have the tendency to switch suppliers, and
- the mindset of the industry is likely to change.

Competitor awareness can be accomplished more formally. Competitor profiling analysis helps you to assess how well you are competing vis-à-vis specific competitors.

The various aspects of competitive advantage can be scored as 'strong', 'average' or 'weak', or alternatively on a 1–5 point scale (see Fig. 2.3) where 5 is 'very strong' and 1 is 'very weak.' Figure 2.3 contains some generic bases for competing which have been implemented successfully in over a hundred companies. (It is important however to tailor these to reflect what is important in your own particular situation.) This

	Very strong 5	Strong 4	Average 3	Weak 2	Very weak 1
Brand image					
Product performance					
Service quality					
Innovation drive					
Cost base					
Supporting systems					
Support skills					

Fig. 2.3 Competitor profiling

analysis needs to be done relative to just one or more key competitors, otherwise it is prone to being superficial and possibly subjective.

In interpreting the criteria in Fig. 2.3, the following points are worth reflecting on:

- *Brand image.* This is not just about brand awareness, but whether this is perceived as an attractive brand halo by customers. (Before its privatization 'British Rail' was a very well-known brand but one which lacked a favourable reputation.)
- *Product performance and value.* This focuses on perceived value for money of the core product.
- *Innovation drive.* This is not just about being innovative, but actually delivering real results from it – either through adding more value to customers or reducing costs, or being able to develop strategically more rapidly.
- *Supporting systems.* These are the IT and non-IT routine processes for delivering value through the organization.
- *Support skills.* These skills comprise general management, commercial, financial, marketing and sales, operations, IT and HR skills.

The choice of which competitor(s) to analyse is an interesting one. This is very far from being self-evident. Killer takeaways on this topic are that you might choose to examine competitors on the following criteria:

- Who represents a likely threat?
- How easy is it for them to attack?
- Is there the potential to learn from them?

The key links to other skills are:

- Acquisitions appraisal (p. 15) – should you buy a competitor?
- Alien thinking (p. 237) – what would an entirely new competitor do?
- Alliances (p. 21) – should you have an alliance with them?
- Business planning (p. 82).
- Market awareness (p. 62).
- Market development (p. 64).
- Option generation (p. 249), e.g. how can you attack them?
- Product development (p. 69).
- Risk and uncertainty analysis (p. 44).
- Selling (p. 72) – especially for tendering.
- Storytelling (p. 47) – about how a competitor may behave in future.
- Strategic thinking (p. 49).

Competitor awareness has a very wide-ranging impact on other key business skills, and is therefore an essential ingredient in an all-round, general manager.

DIVESTMENT

D ivestment is defined as: 'The disposal or closure of all, or part, of the business activities.'

Divestment is far less sexy than acquisitions to many managers, as it is associated with perceived failure. But it can add value (its pros) in a number of ways, for example through:

- the elimination of low-value/value-destroying activities,
- the business being worth more – either in perceived or real terms – to another business, and
- reducing the complexity of your business portfolio, thus enabling you to gain a clearer focus on future strategy development.

The cons are mainly psychological, particularly that divestment:

- may feel like giving up, or failure,
- can be painful in people terms, and
- may seem to limit your future career opportunities.

But where the funds from divestment are reinvested in healthier, value-creating activities, divestment can offer new opportunities for development. For illustration, in the summer of 2003, Manchester United sold the midfielder, David Beckham, for £25 million. The proceeds could be used to buy an extra striker, a midfielder and a defender and still leave change.

Divestment is needed when a business is in severe trouble, or indeed where it has little longer-term hope of increasing shareholder value, under its current ownership. It may also be needed when there are better opportunities simply elsewhere in the business portfolio.

A key technique for evaluating divestment is the strategic option grid (see Fig. 9.2, p.250). Here the grid is used to appraise:

- the 'base case' – how attractive it is to retain the business,
- how it can be further improved with new strategies, and
- how attractive it is to divest.

Killer takeaways on divestment include the following:

- Emphasize the features of the market environment which are attractive to a buyer (especially the growth drivers).
- Identify past competitive strengths and extrapolate out into the future, emphasizing dominance or near-dominance in key segments of the market.
- Identify your future opportunity stream and what it would be worth (as an upside) if you had more funds to invest (i.e. from the acquirer, or from elsewhere).
- Create real or imagined rivalry for the deal and identify to which new parent it would be most worth.
- Plan how we can best convey the impression that we are not in a hurry to do a deal – and we might not need to do one anyway.
- Understand the particular agendas on the acquisition team's minds (especially personal and political agendas), and also how can we exploit 'loose bricks' in the acquisition team's bid strategy.

Links to other key skills include:

- acquisitions and deal-making (p. 18),
- business cases (p. 79) (valuing exit options),
- business planning (p. 82) (to assess the value of retaining the business),
- competitor awareness (p. 25) (for selling to them),
- negotiating (p. 92),
- outsourcing (p. 126) (as a possible vehicle for divestment),
- performance analysis (p. 94) (to diagnose inadequate performance),
- stakeholder management (p. 199) (for influencing your own stakeholders),
- strategic thinking (p. 49),
- storytelling (p. 47), and
- turnaround(p. 158) (to assess any options for retaining the business).

ECONOMIC AWARENESS (MACRO)

 conomic awareness (macro) can be defined as: 'Being aware of the latest trends in the economy, and of the underlying influences on them and of their implications for the business.'

The economy is vulnerable to many factors, including:

- geo-political instability,
- the financial markets,
- the economic cycle, and
- political decisions – especially vis-à-vis fiscal (or taxes and public spending) and monetary policy.

In the new millennium (to date), for example we have seen:

- uncertainty caused by terrorist threat, in the wake of September 11,
- a collapse in the stock markets,
- a second Gulf war, and
- economic slowdown, especially in the formerly booming high-technology sectors.

The pros of having economic awareness are thus that:

- it is helpful for making market and business forecasts,
- it is essential for making strategic investment decisions, whether these be organic or acquisition decisions, and
- it can help in developing competitor strategies which suit a particular kind of trading environment.

Economic awareness is needed continually – it is not something that you can simply turn on in a crisis of business confidence. For example, in

1988 one of the authors worked for one of the big consulting firms. At that time consulting was booming: pay rises were escalating by 10–20 per cent, especially if one was prepared to jump ship and move to another firm. The number of consultants was growing rapidly too – in his imagination he projected that by 2003 about one third of management professionals would be consultants!

Obviously this could not really happen. In 1990 the management consultancy market went over a cliff, caused by the economic slowdown. Consulting firms discounted their rates to keep staff busy (it was rumoured that Price Waterhouse was called Half-Price Waterhouse by some consultants).

Returning to our main theme, in order to understand the economy there are two central techniques that can help. The first is PEST factors, after political, economic, social and technological factors, and the second is growth drivers. PEST factors are shown in Fig. 2.4.

A con of PEST analysis is that it sometimes merely highlights the obvious.

Our second technique is that of growth drivers. Growth drivers (at the level of the economy) are those underlying factors that either generate or inhibit growth in aggregate demand. These drivers can be represented as vectors (see Fig. 2.5).

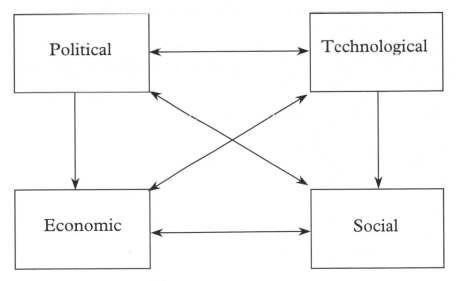

Fig. 2.4 Using PEST analysis

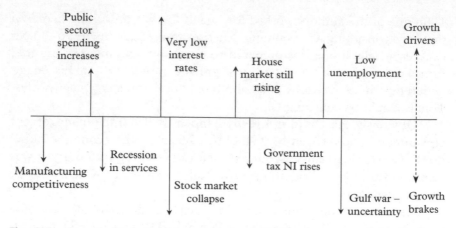

Fig. 2.5 Growth drivers in the economy – early 2003

Figure 2.5 now highlights a not-so-healthy economy. It also suggests that, at least until the end of 2004, the economic environment is likely to be tight, especially should house prices collapse, unemployment increase, and there not be any stock market recovery.

Killer takeaways now include the following considerations:

- Try to think two to three years *ahead* about the economy, (and about specific sectors within it) rather than how it has been over *the past* two to three years.
- Avoid succumbing either to a 'boom' mindset (extrapolating growth into the future), or a 'bust' mindset (assuming that you can't grow in a recession) – it all depends.

Key links to other skills include:

- business planning (p. 15),
- economic awareness (micro) (p. 15),
- financial planning (p. 15)
- global awareness (p. 15)
- helicopter thinking (p. 15)
- risk and uncertainty analysis (p. 15), and
- storytelling (p. 47) (how will the economic environment change?).

ECONOMIC AWARENESS (MICRO)

 conomic awareness (micro) can be defined as: 'An awareness of the economic dynamics and structure of your own market or industry.'

There are two useful techniques for economic awareness (micro):

- growth drivers (those within the market itself), and
- Porter's five competitive forces.

Growth drivers (within a particular market) follow more or less the same model as we explored in the last section on economic awareness (macro).

Growth drivers which are inherent in the market can include a variety of things, for example:

- Service innovation – a new market (or segment) may be more attractive to customers than the existing one, because the need is now delivered in a cheaper or better way.
- Technology innovation – a new technology (for instance, mobile telephones or personal computers) may enable the customer to satisfy previously unmet needs, or needs which were, at best, inadequately served in the past.
- Increased learning about products or services – there may be an increase in awareness among customers that the product or service exists, and how its benefits can be extracted, increasing the frequency of usage.
- Price reductions.
- Scarcity of substitutes – shortages of other means of satisfying needs can generate an (often unsustainable) increase in market or segment growth.

We would stress here that growth drivers are those factors that actually influence the growth in aggregate market demand. To maintain the purity of the technique, external growth driver analysis should not embrace internal growth drivers and brakes.

Taking a graphic example of growth drivers let us examine the growth in the price of dot-com shares 1998–99. Here, the main growth drivers were: the huge growth in usage of the Internet (during 1997–99); the perceived possibilities for reducing costs and thus reducing price (as at Amazon.com); media hype; the rise in dot-com shares, which began to feed on itself, creating a self-fulfilling prophecy; also the 'emperor's clothes syndrome' – no one appeared willing to question the fundamental economic logic of this boom.

The growth drivers of dot-com share prices are shown in Fig. 2.6 (as at 1998–99). But by mid-2000 through to 2001, sentiment had reversed. It would appear that the growth in Internet usage was perhaps a necessary – but not a sufficient – condition of revenue (and margin) generation.

The conditions were not met – and big time.

Figure 2.7 now plots the new growth drivers (and brakes) in late 2000 through to mid-2001. The growth in Internet usage takes on a much lower and weaker importance. The mounting losses of dot-com companies (and in many cases the sheer absence of revenues) reversed sentiment. Once the rot in sentiment had set in, this became a self-fulfilling disaster.

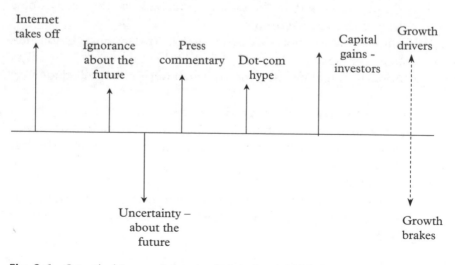

Fig. 2.6 Growth drivers – dot-com market shares 1998–99

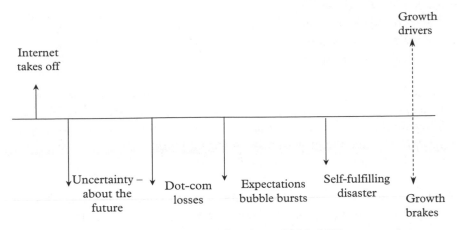

Fig. 2.7   Growth drivers: dot-com market shares 2000–2001

Growth driver analysis has the following pros:

- It helps you to do a reality-check on assumptions of market growth.
- It gives more objective input to potential 'exit' decisions – by checking out whether assumed growth in a market is a reality or merely a mirage.
- It may identify possibilities for actually influencing the growth of the market   rather than just being passive.

Its key cons are potentially:

- that without further research it is subjective, and
- that frequently, in using it, managers merely do a brain-dump of past or present growth drivers, rather than the future.

Another technique is that of Porter's five competitive forces. These are:

- buyer power,
- supplier power,
- entry barriers,
- competitive rivalry, and
- substitutes.

The pros of Porters five competitive forces are that they:

- help identify future structural change in your markets,
- highlight potential reductions in margins,

- can suggest radical strategies for competing more effectively,
- can also be used to analyse the position of your own department, or project, or even yourself within the organization (see Fig. 2.8).

Porter's five forces look at the *quality* of a particular industry or market in terms of the structural factors determining longer-term profitability. They do not look directly at quantitative characteristics, such as market size/growth (see the growth drivers, Figs 2.6 and 2.7).

Five forces cons include the fact that:

- they take the 'industry structure' as a self-contained given – but, in practice, industry boundaries are a good deal more fluid than this, and
- they look somewhat conceptual and abstract, which is a turn-off for many managers.

Killer takeaways on economic awareness (micro) are therefore:

- Think about your *future* growth drivers, your *future* competitive forces, and your *future* basis of competitive advantages.
- Do not see these analyses as givens – you can actively innovate to shape and change your micro-economic environment.

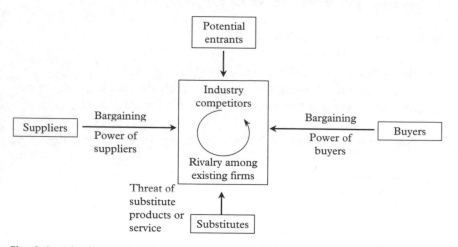

Fig. 2.8 The forces that determine industry profitability

Economic awareness (micro) has a number of links to the other business skills, namely:

- acquisitions appraisal (p. 15) (which potential acquisitions operate in more favourable market environments?),
- business planning (p. 82),
- economic awareness (macro) (p. 30) (the macro environment can have a big impact on economic conditions within a particular market),
- forecasting (p. 156),
- life-cycle management (p. 60),
- market development (p. 64),
- market research (p. 66),
- margin management (p. 88),
- performance analysis (p. 94),
- product development (p. 69),
- risk and uncertainty analysis (p. 44),
- storytelling (p. 47) (future industry dynamics and structure), and
- value management (p. 165) (the micro economic environment has a big impact on creation/destruction of shareholder value).

GLOBAL AWARENESS

 lobal awareness can be defined as: 'Being aware of global influences on your strategy, including markets, competition, economic, regulatory, political, operational, technological and financial.'

Whilst much has been made of global strategy (Bartlett and Ghoshal 1989), markets vary considerably in their exposure to global influences (more 'global' markets include oil, automotives, pharmaceuticals, computers etc.). Markets that have traditionally been less global are those that are more culture-dependent such as retail, but even that is changing.

Suffice it to say that it is increasingly difficult to sustain a career in general management without having significant global awareness.

Global awareness is needed not merely for developing strategies outside your home territory, but also for national strategies too. It would be very unwise to assume that you are safe from competitors with global reach, or who are inclined to expand across borders. The Vikings pioneered the art of quick raids on other countries, and that was a very long time ago!

Global awareness (Yip 1992) breaks down into:

- markets,
- marketing,
- products/services,
- operations,
- competitor moves, and
- governmental relations.

From Yip we therefore see that the question of whether a business is a global one is actually quite complex, and needs to be addressed by breaking down the question into its sub-ingredients.

The pros of having a more global awareness include:

- greater career flexibility – to work in other countries, or in global businesses generally,
- the stimulus of working cross-culturally, and
- without some global awareness, you might find it more difficult to work in industries which are going increasingly global.

A possible con of global awareness is that you may seek global expansion as an end in itself, even though a strategy outside your home terrain may be focused on a less attractive, country market, or you may lack a strong competitive position, or find that the strategy dilutes or destroys, rather than creates shareholder value.

Once again, the strategic option grid (see Fig. 38, p. 250, and 'Option Generation' (p. 249)), is helpful in prioritizing country-by-country attractiveness.

A killer takeaway on global awareness is that when starting out on any new strategy, think about the country which would be best to enter – as if you are landing on the planet earth as an alien – and with lots of money, but freed from the mindset of being in your home country.

Global awareness is now linked to a number of interrelated business skills areas, notably:

- brand management (p. 55) (is it a global brand, or not?),
- cross cultural skills (p. 207),
- economic awareness (macro, p. 30 and micro, p. 33),
- market awareness (p. 62),
- benchmarking (p. 111) (especially your capability against world-class performance standards), and
- helicopter thinking (p. 40) (for example in terms of possible location decisions).

References

Bartlett, C. and Ghoshal, S., (1989) *Managing Across Borders*, Harvard Business School Press, Boston, MA.

Yip, G. (1992) *Total Global Strategy*, Prentice Hall, Englewood Cliffs, NJ.

HELICOPTER THINKING

 elicopter thinking can be defined as: 'Seeing the bigger picture, rather than a specific issue in relative isolation.'

The pros of helicopter thinking are that:

- you don't get too engrossed in relatively less relevant detail,
- you can relate an issue to many others, thus understanding both its significance, and how it can be managed more effectively, and
- you can become far more proactive by anticipating new and perhaps less likely events (see Fig. 2.9).

Helicopter thinking is needed by all, and especially for coping with organizational change.

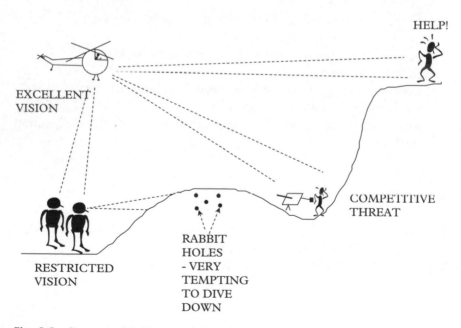

Fig. 2.9 Strategic thinking – as helicopter thinking

A crucial technique for helicopter thinking (over and above Fig. 2.9) is that of the strategic option grid, which we explore in 'Option Generation' (p. 250). The strategic option grid enables you to keep a real-time view of the relative attractiveness, not merely of new options, but also of your existing business activities.

Killer takeaways for helicopter thinking include:

- Use Fig. 2.9 prior to starting any strategy session to emphasize the need to look at the bigger picture, and to avoid descending down the rabbit holes (of excessive detail).
- Whenever a management situation or issue has got very messy, use the idea of helicopter thinking to lift you out of your diagnosis to what you 'really, really want' (sometimes known as the 'Spice Girl' approach to strategy).
- Remember to pay at least as much attention to forces in your external environment as you do to those in your internal environment.

Some key links to other business skills include:

- competitor awareness (p. 25),
- creativity (p. 245),
- customer awareness (p. 57),
- global awareness (p. 38),
- imagination (p. 247) (especially of what might be, as opposed to what is),
- market awareness (p. 62),
- option generation (p. 249),
- problem diagnosis (p. 254) (in order to lift out of this problem, to another thought-space),
- storytelling (p. 47),
- strategic thinking (p. 49) (a more formal structure for applying helicopter thinking).

REGULATORY AWARENESS

 egulatory awareness is defined as: 'Being familiar with existing and emerging regulatory frameworks impacting on your industry or your company, and being aware of their potential implications.'

The pros of regulatory awareness are:

- you will be in a better shape to respond to disruptive or incremental regulatory changes, as they emerge, and
- instead of being caught on the defensive, you will be more able to take the offensive – and be proactive.

Regulatory change is inevitable and can be a major strategic threat. For instance, in early 2002, one of the authors was called upon to consult with a major UK insurance company. The company and, indeed, the whole industry, faced a major upheaval through changes from the governmental regulator into how insurance and other financial services were distributed via independent financial advisers (IFAs).

The co-author was asked to help generate some scenario stories of the industry and how the regulator might seek to impose, or implement change. Happily taking up this challenge, he elected to actually *be the regulator*, or at least to put himself into the mindset and agendas of the regulator, using the 'out-of-body experience'.

By immersing himself in the regulator's agendas and possible intent – particularly by assuming a mindset of being *awesome* – he was able to anticipate most of the radical proposals that the regulator put forward some two months later. Having done these mental gymnastics, and passed on his insight to his client, the client was more able to cope with the disruptive effects.

Regulatory awareness is thus needed when your industry faces significant regulatory change. It is needed not only after this change has been initiated, but also ahead of it, too.

Some useful techniques for coping with regulatory awareness include:

- PEST factors (p. 31) – to consider the interaction between political/regulatory factors with economic, social and technology factors.
- Porter's five forces – to anticipate the effects of regulatory change, for example entry barriers, rivalry, the degree of bargaining power of the buyers, etc.
- Storytelling (and scenarios) – see 'Storytelling' (p. 47).

Some killer takeaways on regulatory awareness are:

- Have the full, 'out-of-body experience' of being the regulator.
- Tell stories about the knock-on effects of a particular regulatory change, especially for its:
  - first order effects,
  - second order effects, and
  - third order effects.
- Anticipate how competitors may respond to such events, again using the out-of-body experience.
- Think about what regulatory environment would be favourable to your own particular company and also how you can try to influence these factors/create them.

Key links to other skills include:

- competitor awareness (p. 25) (how will they behave?),
- cost management (p. 146) (will you need a different cost base?),
- customer awareness (p. 57) (how will their behaviour change?),
- imagination (p. 247) (of what future worlds are a possibility),
- life-cycle management (p. 60),
- margin management (p. 88) (how might margins change?),
- market development (p. 64),
- negotiating (p. 92) (how do you put your case to the regulator?),
- product development (p. 69), and
- storytelling (p. 47).

RISK AND UNCERTAINTY ANALYSIS

R isk can be defined as: 'The possibility of the future state of the world not coming out as hoped for, or as anticipated – and where the probability of this occurring can be estimated.'

Uncertainty can be defined as: 'The possibility of the future state of the world not turning out as hoped for, or as anticipated – but where it is not easy to estimate the probability of this.'

Risk and uncertainty make management more interesting, exciting and ultimately, personally lucrative: after all, if neither existed then why would there be any kind of premium in pay over a non-management job?

Risk and uncertainty analysis is needed whenever the future is unpredictable, whether this is externally, internally or both. Risk and uncertainty analysis is needed for new product launch/market development, acquisitions, alliances, project appraisal and project management, change management, etc.

A central technique for managing both risk and uncertainty is the uncertainty grid, which is derived from Mitroff and Linstone, 1993. Using this grid, managers can plot the key assumptions driving the value of any decision. These can be external and internal, soft and hard assumptions.

Having selected a subset of these assumptions, these are now prioritized by using the grid (which can be a flip chart, a white board, or a piece of paper). Once assumptions are carefully and skilfully defined, it is possible to debate the relative importance and uncertainty of these various assumptions (using a flip chart, the assumptions can be easily moved around using Post-it® notes).

These assumptions are defined in terms of 'the future world being okay'. For example, if we were using it to understand the uncertainties of getting to a meeting in London on time, assumptions would be defined as 'the trains will run on time', rather than 'the trains will not run on time'.

A frequent mistake (when first using the grid) is to have some assumptions defined positively and some negatively. This usually makes it impossible to judge the overall downsides to a strategy. An example of this would be 'Kings Cross Station might be closed' (a negative assumption) and 'there will be no London Underground strike that day' (a positive assumption).

At the beginning of the appraisal, key assumptions are likely to be mapped in the due north and northeast quadrants. Upon testing it is quite common to find one or more assumptions moving over to the danger zone in the southeast.

Figure 2.10 actually relates to the new product launch. The extra sales volume from existing customers is very important, but also considered relatively certain. Sales to new customers are considerably more uncertain (but also very important) – shown in the southeast of the grid. Product launch costs are somewhat less important and also reasonably certain (shown just slightly northeast of the centre of the grid).

Killer takeaways on risk and uncertainty include:

- Beware doing sensitivity analysis without a full risk and uncertainty assessment first. Only once this is done, preferably using the uncertainty gird, should you decide whether to consider a five, ten or twenty per cent variance from your expectations.
- Do not ignore any assumption which is both (potentially) very uncertainty and very important – this will probably come back to haunt you!

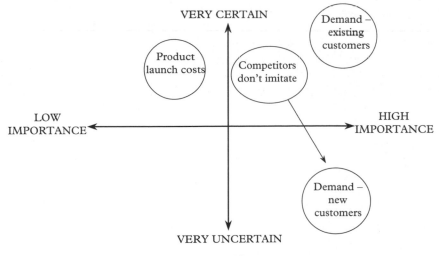

Fig. 2.10 The uncertainty/importance grid

Key linkages with other business skills include:

- acquisitions appraisal (p. 15),
- alliances (p. 21),
- change management (p. 173),
- competitor awareness (p. 25),
- forecasting (p. 156),
- imagination (p. 247),
- market development (p. 64), and
- product development (p. 69).

Reference

Mitroff, I.I. & Linstone, H.A. (1993) *The Unbounded Mind*, Oxford University Press, Oxford.

STORYTELLING

Storytelling about the future is a particularly powerful skill for 'seeing around corners'.

Scenarios in storytelling need to:

- be internally consistent views of the future,
- focus on discontinuity and change (not on continuity), and
- explore how the underlying systems in the business environment may generate change.

Scenarios give views of how the competitive players (existing and new) might behave. They are not static and comprehensive views of the future. Scenarios are in many ways more like a video film – they are of necessity selective but contain a dynamic storyline. They thus contain a series of views (pictures) of the future. This is fruitfully presented as a series of pictures, not as a single one. Also, there is a storyline, which enables these pictures to hang together.

The story can be run (again like a video film) forward or, alternatively, backward. By replaying the story you can work backwards from a particular scenario to see what events might bring about a particular outcome. (These events are called 'transitional events'.)

Just as 'strategy' is frequently defined as a being a pattern in a stream of (past and current) decisions, so a 'scenario' is a pattern of future events, and of the interaction between customers, competitors and other key players in the industry. It is then brought alive by storytelling.

Storytelling (scenario) pros are:

- it helps you anticipate the future,
- it helps you to be more proactive, and
- it makes your strategies more resilient.

The possible cons are that:

- many managers find it hard to do storytelling (even though they probably do this for their children), and
- scenarios are sometimes reduced to the status of forecasts, which is not their real purpose.

Scenarios can help in a number of ways. Scenario planning at Shell is principally known for its very 'big picture' analysis – particularly for global or industry-broad scenarios, or for country-specific scenarios. In addition, managers can also perform issue-specific scenarios (for example the impact of regulatory/environmental pressure). Or one can do scenarios specific to a particular decision.

Scenarios can thus be used for:

- acquisitions and alliances,
- strategic investment decisions,
- strategic projects,
- strategic change,
- organizational change, and
- your own personal career.

The most useful technique for developing scenarios/stories about the future we will meet in the forthcoming section 'Risk and Uncertainty Analysis' – in the form of the uncertainty grid (Fig. 2.10, p. 45).

Killer takeaways:

- Work backwards from the future to see which events (transitional events) would have to occur in order to crystallize that particular world, and how these events were brought about.
- Never try to be right or accurate with storytelling. The point is simply to explore the future.

Key links with other skills are:

- brainstorming (p. 239),
- business planning (p. 82),
- creativity (p. 245),
- imagination (p. 249),
- questioning (of assumptions) (p. 258), and
- risk and uncertainty analysis (p. 44).

STRATEGIC THINKING

S trategic thinking can be defined as: 'defining your strategic position, your options and also their implementation issues in order to arrive at the "cunning plan".' (Grundy and Brown 2002)

The cunning plan has its origins in *Blackadder*, the TV comedy series featuring Rowan Atkinson (whose cunning has led him to amass a £60 million fortune, personally).

As an example of a 'cunning plan' in the *Blackadder* millennium video, Blackadder and Baldrick invent a time machine. Before they are ready to set off, one of them falls on the controls, sending them back into the past.

Unfortunately they cannot remember the original time settings, and although they are enjoying themselves disrupting the past, eventually want to get back to the present. In frustration, Blackadder says to Baldrick,

'So I am condemned to spend the rest of my life in a small room with two toilets, with the stupidest man on earth.'

To which Baldrick replies:

'Don't worry, because I think I have a cunning plan.'

To which Blackadder says,

'I am sceptical. What is your "cunning plan"?'

Baldrick outlines his plan:

'You know how when people drown, their life flashes back in front of their eyes. If you were to stick your head in a bucket of water, just until the moment you were about to die, then you would remember the settings, and we could all go home.'

'A cunning plan,' says Blackadder, 'With one or two minor improvements …'

And in the next scene we see Blackadder putting Baldrick's head down the toilet. Not content with Baldrick's cunning plan, Blackadder has made this into a 'stunning plan'.

A cunning plan typically has the following features:

* It starts off with the objective – 'what do I really, really want?' – in this case, remembering the settings.
* It brings together some possible solutions in a novel combination – for looking at how you might remember something you have forgotten. At least one of these solutions is relatively surprising – it certainly is not an obvious solution.
* It is relatively simple at bottom.
* It is relatively hard for others to imitate.

For example, one of the authors visited the British Grand Prix at Silverstone. He and his son James were running late for the Saturday qualifiers. They shot out of their car (without checking their exact location). On their return later that day they came out of what looked like the same exit (but it wasn't). As they had entered the car park from a different angle they could not locate their car – indeed they were actually looking in the wrong place in a sea of cars.

After fifteen minutes and getting increasingly desperate they looked for assistance from one of the stewards, who suggested a not-so-cunning plan.

'You can't find your car?' he said.

'No.'

'What kind of car is it?' he asked.

'It's an Audi A4, dark red,'

'What is its registration number,' he then asked.

'N151 SPE.'

Pausing for a moment he then said, 'Maybe if you walked around you could see if you could spot it.'

They rolled their eyes and resumed the long search ... Finally they realized they had come out of a different exit and found the car. On the journey home, as an amusing piece of in-car entertainment, they both brainstormed more cunning plans for how they might have found it (see the box below).

Eleven cunning ways for finding their car

1   Borrowing a very large ladder from Octagon who run the Grand Prix.
2   Climbing up the mobile phone aerial (adjacent to the car park with a radioactive-proof suit).
3   Going on the big wheel adjacent to the car park.
4   Asking to take over from one of the cameramen who track the Grand Prix with telescopic cameras mounted on incredibly tall platforms.
5   Climbing on the roof of one of the more central cars – without damaging it.
6   Chartering a helicopter (at £1000 an hour).
7   Parachuting down on the car park (a bit dangerous, though).
8   Waiting until all the cars had gone (perhaps not-so-cunning this one).
9   Calling in the SAS to home in on our car with laser sights.
10 Contacting the Pentagon to obtain high resolution/magnified pictures of the car park (either by Blackbird spy-plan or by spy satellite).
11 Bribing the steward £200 to call in his entire team to help them to find it (the best one – very simple).

The above example illustrates:

- the need for creative and innovative thinking in developing a strategy and not merely analysis, and
- the equal need to be creative in challenging constraints and in acquiring the deploying resources – for competitive advantage.

The pros of strategic thinking (and of the 'cunning plan') are that:

- it helps us to be more imaginative about what is possible – both in the industry, and for ourselves,
- it can give one major competitive advantage and generate significant extra shareholder value – in its own right (Grundy & Brown 2002), and
- it can get us out of some (otherwise) tight spots.

The only possible con of strategic thinking is that it is mistaken for pure 'blue-sky' thinking, which is impractical and will never actually happen (but this is a misconception of what 'strategic thinking' actually entails).

The strategic option grid (see the section on 'Option Generation', Fig. 9.2, p. 250) is probably the most effective technique for strategic thinking.

Killer takeaways include:

- To spend an hour a week in a meeting with yourself to do some strategic thinking (book it into your diary as a 'meeting' – so you cannot be disturbed).
- In that session, focus on just *one* issue at a time.
- Remember not merely to diagnose it, but also to consider where you 'really, really, really want to be?' (The 'Spice Girls' approach to strategy.)
- Remember too that not only are there likely to be many different options (for *what* you can do, but also for *how* you do it (the 'Kama Sutra' approach).

The key links to other business skills now include:

- alien thinking (p. 237),
- business planning (p. 82),
- creativity (p. 245),
- helicopter thinking (p. 40),
- imagination (p. 247),
- option generation (p. 249), and
- storytelling (p. 47).

Reference

Grundy, A.N. & Brown, L. (2002) *Be Your Own Strategy Consultant*, Thomson Learning, London.

Marketing Skills

BRAND MANAGEMENT

rand management can be defined as: 'The management of the brand life cycle from launch to development and right through to its rejuvenation – both in terms of its external positioning and brand values, and in terms of internal behaviours.'

The pros of brand management are:

- it ensures clarity and consistency of competitive positioning,
- it helps to exploit the economic value-creating potential of the brand, and
- it helps differentiate the company's products, promotions and price premium, to avoid discounting, and increases customer loyalty and thus switching costs.

Possible cons include the fact that, as a process, it may become an end in itself, and an industry in its own right.

Brand management is needed whenever there is a significant heritage from a past superior product or service delivery. It is particularly relevant to products and/or services that stand for something distinctive (often called the 'brand values'). For example the Guinness brand stands for strength and healthiness – symbolized in its brilliant advertisements, which end with the word: 'Believe'.

Brand management is needed at all stages of organic product/market development. Even where the product is relatively mature, or even in decline, it is still needed. For example, in the early 2000s the fashion brand Pringle was rejuvenated. Marks & Spencer has also tried to rejuvenate its brand in a similar fashion through the injection of new life with sub-brands like Per Una, Blue Harbour and Agent Provocateur, with some degree of success.

Brand management is also needed during the integration phase of any acquisition – in order to either strengthen an acquired brand, to replace it, or to begin its migration towards a new name.

A killer takeaway for brand management is that the organizational behaviours supporting the brand (especially service) *must* be consistent with it, or the brand values will be tarnished.

For example, the Rover 75 brand, under BMW's ownership in the late 1990s, had very unclear targeting, resulting in a huge backlog of unsold cars, which Jeremy Clarkson, leading TV car pundit, characterized as: 'The Rover 75 when it was launched presented serious problems for air-traffic controllers – the runaways of airfields were full of them' (this was where their unsold models – in their hundreds, were parked).

Where underlying behaviours are not currently consistent with the brand, then major culture change is needed. Brands are not just about marketing and products, they are equally about aligning people and their behaviours with the brand.

Brands only have a meaning if they are targeted at particular segments of the market.

Key links to other skills include:

- acquisitions integration (p. 107),
- competitor awareness (p. 25),
- customer awareness (p. 57),
- life-cycle management (p. 60),
- market research (p. 66), and
- product development (p. 69).

References

Doyle, P. (1994) *Marketing Management and Strategy*, Prentice Hall, Hemel Hempstead.

Kotler, P. (1984) *Marketing Management*, Prentice Hall, Englewood Cliffs, NJ.

CUSTOMER AWARENESS

C ustomer awareness can be defined as: 'Being able to have the out-of-body experience of managing you or the customer and how he/she perceived the value you add or are destroying, and on a segment-by-segment basis.'

The pros of customer awareness are that:

- it is the starting point (often) for successful strategy development,
- it can give you a major edge over your competitors, and
- by delivering superior customer value, and by avoiding destroying customer value, you will find it much easier to retain customers, to build market share, and to gain share from your competitors.

An invaluable technique for enhancing customer awareness is to use a technique called 'motivators and hygiene factors'. Hygiene factors are the basic standards of product and service delivery which, unless delivered well, will destroy value. Where hygiene factors are not met they detract from value – and from the buying impulse. Motivator activities excite customers distinctively, and are the key sources of differentiation.

In Fig. 3.1 the conventional 'enabling' forces become the motivators, and the 'constraining' forces become the hygiene factors not being met. The relative size of the arrow (or vector) is a visual indicator of the actual strength of motivators and hygiene factors (from a customer's perspective). This tool can be used either to help predict customer buying behaviour, or for benchmarking customer value added by the firm.

You will need to think through these questions:

- Is the factor really a motivator or merely a hygiene factor? (Often, managers put in 'motivators' things which are simply hygiene factors met to different degrees.)
- How important is that motivator or hygiene factor?
- How well is it met (or is it not met at all)?

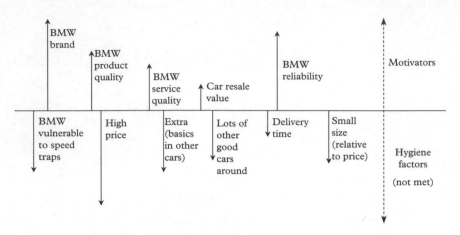

Fig. 3.1 Motivator/hygiene factor analysis – businessman contemplating a BMW purchase

The motivator/hygiene factor analysis clearly needs to be checked out by some empirical research – with customers.

The pros of motivator/hygiene factor analysis include:

- it gives you an outside-in perspective on your competitive advantage,
- it prioritizes customer value both in terms of importance and the extent to which value is being created (or, indeed, destroyed), and
- it allows you to think ahead about future value creation in the industry, thus pre-empting your competitors.

Its cons might include that it can become too subjective unless one is fully capable of having the 'out-of-body-experience', and unless at least some market data is collected.

Killer takeaways from customer awareness:

- Besides having your out-of-body experience of *existing* customer needs, also anticipate what future/latent needs might be.
- Use motivator/hygiene factor analysis whenever tendering for business.

The linkages of customer awareness with other skills include:

- competitor awareness (in order to prioritize aspects of competing) (p. 107),
- life-cycle management (p. 25),
- market awareness (p. 62),
- market development (p. 64),
- market research (p. 66),
- negotiating (p. 92),
- product development (p. 69), and
- selling (p. 72).

References

Grundy, A.N. & Brown, L. (2002) *Be Your Own Strategy Consultant*, Thomson Learning, London.

LIFE-CYCLE MANAGEMENT

L ife-cycle management' can be defined as: 'Managing the life cycle of products, markets, customers, distribution channels, technologies and know-how in order to meet, and to anticipate, market needs.'

Life-cycle management typically involves managing some, or all of these variables in terms of:

* incubation,
* growth,
* launch,
* maturity,
* decline, and
* rejuvenation.

Its pros are:

* it draws attention to the need to vary your strategy, your resources and your mindset over various life cycles, and
* it emphasizes that maturity is not necessarily an endgame, but may be merely a stepping stone to rejuvenation.

But a con is that it can encourage managers to think myopically of the stage that they are currently in, or prevent thoughts of potential rejuvenation, or the incubation of new ideas.

Life-cycle management is needed for the following:

* Products/services which almost inevitably move through these life-cycle stages.
* The account management of customers whose needs may change over time. Also it is relevant where key stakeholders (in a business-to-business context) may personally reach saturation of these products/services, or may even move on from their current roles.

- Understanding the industry life cycle, particularly as the market growth drivers and also Porter's five competitive forces change, and the relevance of the company's mindset and competencies.

An example of life-cycle management is that of project management as a product. In the late 1990s, project management consulting and training was in a healthy growth mode. This was triggered in part by management's need to deal with the increased rate of change, and also by the availability of software packages – like that of Microsoft Project. This growth was further increased by a finalized methodology called 'PRINCE', which gave managers some structure for managing projects.

By 2002/2003 many new entrants had come into the project management training and consultancy market. But, the basis of project management had still not fundamentally changed, making it easy for new entrants to deliver a current, state-of-the art project management programme.

As a result of these influences, project management training had become more or less a commodity. Mindful of these shifts in life-cycle changes, the authors have developed a more sophisticated and relevant product and process called 'strategic project management', which integrates strategic analysis, implementation strategy and conventional project management into a more powerful process. Our objective was to proactively manage this project's life cycle through innovation. Our next step is hopefully to persuade Microsoft (a client) to build in these techniques to their software (or, on second thoughts, might this commoditize it?).

A killer takeaway from life-cycle management is that you should never assume that something is forever. A 'frozen' strategy will ultimately get found out, however awesome and dominant you may appear at a particular stage.

The links to other techniques include:

- competitor awareness (p. 25),
- customer awareness (p. 57),
- margin management (p. 88),
- market awareness (p. 62),
- organization and people planning (p. 220),
- product development (p. 69), and
- strategic thinking (p. 49).

MARKET AWARENESS

arket awareness can be defined as: 'Having an intuitive understanding of market needs, market change, and why this change is occurring.'

Its pros are:

- it should help to prevent you from becoming complacent,
- it will increase readiness to change, especially in your resource base and mindset, and
- it ought to suggest new and exciting avenues for strategy development.

A possible con is that you may be mistaken about trends because you have made assumptions which you may not have checked out.

Market awareness is needed particularly at times of significant market change. For example, in the late 1990s Marks & Spencer seemed to have failed to have appreciated that:

- many of its potential customers didn't want just the standard, not-so-fashionable, M&S brand, and
- because of new, lower-cost competition, existing customers were expecting similar value, rendering M&S's past formula of 'value-for-money' – based mainly on UK-sourced clothing – obsolescent.

The result of this mistake was almost £0.5 billion wiped off its operating profits by around 2000.

The most relevant techniques for market awareness have already been covered, namely:

- PEST factors,
- growth drivers,
- Porter's five competitive forces, and
- motivator/hygiene factors.

Killer takeaway: if asked the question 'what business are you in?', you may reply that you are in a large number of businesses spanning geographic markets, industry markets, types of customer, distribution method – so begin by mapping out what these actually are, and might be.

The links with other key skills include:

- business planning (p. 82),
- customer awareness (p. 57),
- market development (p. 64),
- market research (p. 66), and
- market segmentation (p. 90).

MARKET DEVELOPMENT

Market development can be defined as: 'The proactive process of exploiting existing, new and latent market opportunities for financial advantage.'

Market development should also be a highly proactive process – markets do not stay still so rather than just responding to change why not to play a more active role in developing your market?

A classic example of proactive market development was that of Dyson Appliances in the mid/late 1990s. Dyson revolutionized the carpet cleaning market with a bagless machine that was also stylish and upmarket. As a result of these innovations Dyson achieved dominance of the UK market, and expanded the market with its (and its competitors') higher-priced machines.

The pros of market development are that:

- it rejuvenates the company,
- it provides avenues to potentially profitable growth, and
- it is a stimulus to organizational energy, and is motivating.

A potential con of market development is that it can entail diversifying into areas where existing competencies are less appropriate.

Market development (as a process) is relevant to organic strategies, to acquisitions, and of course to alliances.

Market development can be closely or less closely related to current markets. The more distant or different these markets are, the more the company needs to be aware of the dangers of diversification. For example, Dyson Appliances decided to enter the US market with its premium-priced product at over $400. The US market is notoriously difficult to compete in, and often requires major adjustments in mindset. As of 2003, the jury is out on whether Dyson will or won't be successful here.

You have already seen most critical techniques (for example, growth drivers, Porter's five forces, and the motivator/hygiene factors), and the strategic option grid too (see the later section on option generation).

Its links with other key business skills include:

- acquisitions (p. 15),
- alliances (p. 21),
- business planning (p. 82),
- competitor awareness (p. 25),
- customer awareness (p. 57),
- forecasting (p. 156),
- life-cycle management (p. 60),
- market awareness (p. 62),
- market research (p. 66), and
- product development (p. 69).

MARKET RESEARCH

 arket research can be defined as: 'The systematic, but often intuitive methodology of establishing customers' present and future needs, in order to match these up with one's own products and services.'

Market research has two key pros:

- it diminishes the reliance on subjective perceptions of customer needs, and
- it can tease out not only current, but future (and latent/needs) too.

But set against this are the cons:

- it can become a very expensive and/or a time-consuming operation – because its advocates often propose larger data samples in order to preserve statistical validity, and
- the data gathered may not be particularly insightful, or may be limited primarily to *present* customer needs, rather than to future needs.

Market research (of some form or another) is needed for all new product/ market development. But it should also, (at least in some abbreviated form) be an input into business plans, and especially into any full blown strategic review. It is equally important during acquisition appraisal, as customers can give you some most interesting insights into the relative strength/weakness of a potential acquisition, and about its products, its services and its culture.

Market research can be highly quantitative, qualitative or both. Traditional approaches to market research tend to favour more quanti-tatively-based methods, with skilfully worded questionnaires containing response parameters such as:

- strongly agree,
- agree,
- neither agree nor disagree,
- disagree, and
- strongly disagree.

The authors' contention is that these methodologies *can* be taken too far at times. In their view it needs to be more focused on real insights – not only about *what* customers need and *how well* they see current products/services being delivered but more importantly *why* they have these perceptions, and what is their *real significance.*

Taking this point to perhaps absurdity, imagine spending a lovely evening with a new girlfriend/boyfriend and not managing to escape their bedroom before morning. The very next day you get your market research form out and ask: 'Did you enjoy last night with me darling? I am doing some market research: Do you strongly agree, agree, neither agree nor disagree etc. ...'

Qualitative market research based on deeper study of a smaller number of decision-makers (and of their agendas and perceptions) might, therefore, be more effective.

For instance, when helping a major supermarket chain develop its home shopping business in the 1990s one of the authors interviewed his wife (now ex) in the back garden.

'Ann, what would you pay for a home shopping delivery?' he asked.

'I dunno,' she responded.

'What would turn you on or off about home shopping?'

'I dunno,' she responded.

(His hypothesis at that stage was that 20 million other female house-holders would probably not know either.) As he was turning away, she then said, on reflection:

'But I will tell you that if they are five minutes late, especially if I am doing the school run, that would be the end of the relationship.' (She meant with the supermarket, not with him.)

From this he concluded that a) the grocery home shopping market place needed to be educated about the value of home shopping; b) the supermarket might, if it succeeded in a), charge for the service; and c) good logistics was going to be absolutely crucial.

A hundred questionnaires in the traditional mode of market research might have failed to produce this valuable insight.

Killer takeaways on market research are:

- Remember what you are trying to achieve, and seek to achieve this goal with the most cunning and insightful market research techniques.
- Before you ever commission external or internal market research, conduct some 'psychic market research' first: ask yourself 'given these questions, what would I be almost certainly likely to find out – even if I did not do market research? (This can be eighty per cent accurate – and a lot cheaper! – as long as your intuitions are well grounded.) (Could we ask you not to point out this suggestion to colleagues at Cranfield School of Management in the marketing group?)

Key links to other skills include:

- life-cycle management (p. 60),
- market development (p. 64), and
- product development (p. 69).

PRODUCT DEVELOPMENT

P roduct development can be defined as: 'The process of developing an existing or new product in order to satisfy existing customers needs better, or to meet new customer needs.'

Product development is normally associated with external products, but can be applied to internal products too. For example, when launching a new management development programme it is possible to:

- brand it,
- launch it with a half-day conference with the CEO/future tutors, and
- support it with merchandise and videos,

as did one leading healthcare company in the UK.

So product development can also be a process applied to an internal service. The pros of product development are that it:

- continually updates the product portfolio of a business,
- helps to grow the business, and
- hopefully, achieves a higher margin mix of products.

Possible cons are that:

- the market needs are not fully thought through,
- now products may make operations more complex to support and may have marginal benefit, actually destroying, rather than creating, shareholder value.

It is often said that nine out of ten product ideas fail. But, inevitably, many products do not pass the 'proof of concept' stage, so that estimation is probably a little harsh. Hopefully, once proved conceptually, most products then go on to succeed.

Product development is needed not merely for organic development but also for getting the value out of acquisition integration – which might entail significant further investment to develop the business. Without product development you may well find yourself being overtaken by competitors.

Besides the strategy and marketing techniques already covered (especially motivator/hygiene factors), a further technique is called 'wishbone analysis'. Taking Dyson Appliances bagless carpet cleaner as an example we start at the very left with Dyson's vision 'Dyson Beats Hoover'. The bones of the wishbone (in no particular order) contain the alignment factors that were both *necessary and sufficient* for achieving that result. These include not merely our product delivery, but also customer motivator/hygiene factors, competitor reaction and other aligned conditions externally (see Fig. 3.2).

By using this pictorial representation to capture all aspects of the *system* of alignment (Senge 1990), there is perhaps more chance of success. The 'wishbone' can be tested for resilience by putting each of the bones/alignment factors on the uncertainty grid (see Fig. 2.10, p.45).

Killer takeaways from product development are:

- Always work backwards from the customers and not from what you happen to feel like doing.
- Always ask (within the 'wishbone' alignment factors), what is the one big thing you have forgotten? – like 'competitors' mindsets won't change'.

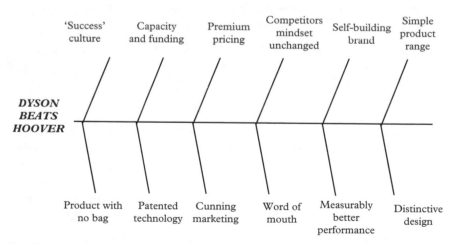

Fig. 3.2 Wishbone analysis

- Practice the art of 'psychic market research' (see earlier section Customer Awareness p. 57) or collect some rich data on your customers through a very small sample, early on.

Links to other skills now include:

- competitor awareness,
- customer awareness,
- imagination,
- market development,
- market research,
- risk and uncertainty analysis, and
- strategic thinking.

References

Senge, P. (1990) *The Fifth Discipline: The Art & Practice of the Learning Organization*, Doubleday, New York.

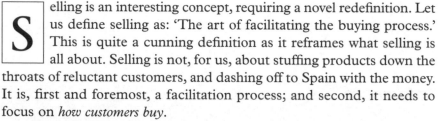

SELLING

Selling is an interesting concept, requiring a novel redefinition. Let us define selling as: 'The art of facilitating the buying process.' This is quite a cunning definition as it reframes what selling is all about. Selling is not, for us, about stuffing products down the throats of reluctant customers, and dashing off to Spain with the money. It is, first and foremost, a facilitation process; and second, it needs to focus on *how customers buy*.

A wonderfully entertaining book on this theme is Geoff Burch's *Resistance is Useless*, which contains entertaining stories of how, for instance, you might sell a tank to Genghis Khan – who would not know what one looked like. You would have to work backwards from *his* mindset, not simply assuming that a tank would just slot in neatly to his plans.

The cons of the conventional selling concept (conceived of as a way of ensuring that your planned product is actually consumed by customers) are:

- it can be experienced as 'pushy' by customers – as a turn off,
- it will increase their defensiveness, and will increase barriers to decision-making,
- it will cause a protracted buying process, and
- if successful, a dissatisfied customer may not buy again from you.

The pros of the idea of selling as a facilitated buying process are:

- It gives customers more of a feeling of control, allowing them to relax and to buy.
- It allows you to listen to their needs, to fine-tune your product/service, to thereby increase value added and build switching costs.
- It builds, rather than destroys relationships (in a business-to-business environment).

Even in consumer marketing, which cannot be so tailored, it is essential to model your sales effort wholly along the lines of 'how does a customer make a decision to buy?'.

'Selling' (as redefined by us) is needed more often in management than perhaps is appreciated. We are not just talking about selling externally to a key account, but also selling management ideas/projects, too.

One technique for analysing the buying process is AIDA (A for awareness; I for interest; D for desire; and A for action).

The idea here is that you can create awareness (but without real interest), or achieve both but with no real desire, and even when desire occurs, you may still get inaction. The corollary of this is that to make a sale it is often better to work intensively to facilitate a small number of customers *all the way along* the buying process – to achieve crystallization of demand, rather than to scatter-gun your efforts. (As independent management consultants, both of us know how true this is! If we did not practise this, we would be probably out on the London streets at weekends – begging.)

In terms of the business-to-business market or internal selling within the company, further (and more elaborate, but effective) frameworks include the buying/selling cycles as shown below. Here we see the buyer has to move around a complex cycle (Fig. 3.3), which is supported by his/her adviser (Fig. 3.4). In selling an idea internally there is often an even *higher attrition* rate of ideas than when selling externally, so patience, stealth, accuracy and sensitivity are even more paramount.

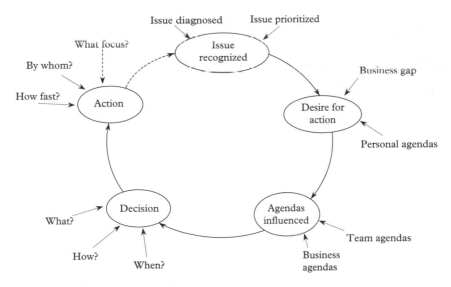

Fig. 3.3 The buying cycle – the customer

A further useful technique is that of wishbone analysis, which we saw in the section 'Product Development' (p. 70) to identify all the necessary and sufficient conditions required in order to make a bargaining decision.

Killer takeaways include:

- Selling is facilitating the buying process, not making a pushy sale (Fig. 3.4).
- Always work backwards from the customers' agendas – have the out-of-body experience.
- Remember, what is the one big thing we have forgotten which might prevent the customer from buying?

Key links to other skills include:

- business cases (p. 79) (giving the customer a business case for his/her purchase),
- competitor awareness (p. 25),
- creativity (p. 245),
- customer awareness (p. 57),
- empathizing (p. 182) (with the customer),
- listening (p. 190) (to the customer),
- networking (p. 216),
- political awareness (p. 196),
- risk and uncertainty analysis (p. 44),

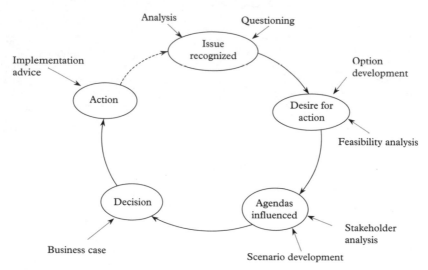

Fig. 3.4   The buying cycle – the adviser

- stakeholder management,
- storytelling, and
- value management (to put an economic value on the product – from the customer perspective).

(Notice that we are now increasingly entering the land of softer skills, for example with 'political awareness' and 'stakeholder management'.)

Reference

Burch, G. (2002) *Resistance is Useless,* Capstone Publishing, Oxford.

Commercial Management Skills

BUSINESS CASES

business case can be defined as: 'A reasoned argument for making an investment in a business which is based on a clear strategy and with a full appreciation of the resources needed, of the risks and of the returns.'

The pros of making a business case are:

- It helps you to think through the issues involved in making the investment, and also the options and the strategy for implementing it.
- It helps to ensure that the project is more likely to beat its hurdle rate of return.
- It will help to gain approval to go ahead.
- By discussion with senior management, also should challenge its assumptions, as well as building its potential for return, it ought to increase likely returns/reduce risks.

One possible con is that business cases are sometimes compiled purely as 'selling documents', without full exploration of risks and downsides.

A business case is needed for:

- acquisitions,
- alliances,
- major organic investment (e.g. market, product, technology),
- infrastructure investment (IT, restructuring, change management), and
- divestment.

The relevant techniques include:

- For external strategies – the strategy tools which we have already covered (e.g. growth drivers, five forces, motivator/hygiene factors, competitor profiling, wishbone analysis etc.).

- For all investment decisions – the uncertainty grid (already covered).
- For financial evaluation – discounted cash flow/payback (Grundy 2002b).
- Stakeholder analysis (see 'Stakeholder Management', p. 199).

Discounted cash flow works on the basis that money in the future is worth less than money now. So, for example, if I invest £10,000 now and get £5000 net cash flow over each of the next three years (and my cost of capital is 10%) the value to us now will be:

$$\text{Net present value} = -£10,000 + \frac{£5000}{1.1} + \frac{£5000}{(1.1) \times (1.1)}$$

$$+ \frac{£5000}{(1.1) \times (1.1) \times (1.1)}$$

$$= £12,433 - £10,000$$

$$= £2433$$

(A net present value is 'the *present value* of future net cash flows less the initial outlay'.)

The 'payback' is the duration over which the initial investment is recouped – in the above case just two years, as there is annual cash flow of £5000, and an outlay of £10,000.

Killer takeaways now include:

- Never do sensitivity analysis before using the uncertainty grid on your key assumptions – try not to do plus or minus five or ten per cent in more 'insensitivity analysis' – as you will be just trying to get to the right answer.
- In the business case, have the out-of-body experience, working backwards from the internal stakeholders' agendas.

The following format can be used for a business case:

- executive summary (1 page),
- project definition, objectives and scope (1 page),

- how the project adds value (new opportunity, tangible synergies, defensive or protective value) (1 page),
- key external and internal assumptions (with an evaluation of importance and uncertainty) (3 pages),
- implementation issues (1 page), and
- summary financials (1 page).

This brings the total length to 8 pages plus detailed appendices containing technical details, detailed financial and non-financial measures and milestones, detailed financial sensitivities, detailed resource requirements – possibly another 7 pages. This brings a typical case to just 15 pages.

Links to other skills include:

- building (p. 241),
- business planning (p. 82),
- challenging (p. 243),
- economic awareness (macro, p. 30 and micro, p. 33),
- helicopter and strategic thinking (p. 40 and p. 49),
- life-cycle management (p. 60),
- option generation (p. 249),
- problem diagnosis (p. 254),
- project appraisal (p. 98),
- questioning (p. 258),
- report writing (p. 227),
- risk and uncertainty analysis (p. 44),
- storytelling (p. 47),
- stakeholder management (p. 199),
- summarizing (p. 202), and
- value management (p. 165).

Reference

Grundy, A.N. (2002) *Shareholder Value*, Capstone Publishing, Oxford.

BUSINESS PLANNING

usiness planning is the process of diagnosing, evaluating, prioritizing and programming ideas and actions for improving business performance, and for developing capability.

The key pros of business planning are that it:

- provides a framework for ongoing strategy development and review,
- gives managers a tangible guide for action, with parameters about what is expected of them,
- sets a framework for rewards, and
- gives (hopefully) a greater emphasis to shareholder value.

Some cons of business planning are that:

- it can be too time consuming and bureaucratic,
- once completed, plans are not always actively referred to,
- plans often contain lots of goals ('why?' and 'what?') but relatively little real implementation planning ('how?'),
- the plans are often under-resourced, or resources are spread too thinly, and
- they frequently focus too much on the financials, and less on competitive position, capability development, and on innovation.

Business plans are needed not merely for outward-facing business units (and also at the divisional and corporate levels), but equally by internal services. After all, if internal services deliver value, shouldn't they have business plans, too? Indeed, an individual manager himself/herself ought to have their own business plans for their own role.

Many of the relevant external techniques for business planning have been covered in the section on strategy (p. 13). Gap analysis is an essential technique, too (Ansoff 1969).

Gap analysis is one of the least well-used tools of strategic analysis. It is still quite rare (even in the new millennium) to see it in formal use. Frequently, corporate plans are based more on aggregating separate, tactical plans for achieving more profit, rather than by creating challenging, but completely viable, business strategies.

An example of gap analysis for a maturing company is illustrated in Fig. 4.1. Here we see the core business activities facing competitive pressure and a fall in growth rate, squeezing operating profit. Although international development and new business activities may fill part of corporate aspirations, there still remains a significant gap.

Whilst gap analysis can be very useful – if not essential – unless it is coupled with additional techniques of an earlier strategic analysis it is likely to be optimistic and unsupported by robust strategies based on solid competitive advantage.

Indeed, in certain industries, managers have been known to just throw ideas – almost at random – into 'the gap'. Jokingly, we refer to this sometimes as 'CRAP analysis', (CReating Artificial Plans) to signify that, all too often, initiatives aimed at filling the strategic gap are not thought through.

The key pros of gap analysis are that it:

- provides a very clear focus for sketching your aspirations for the business,
- links in with the strategic breakthroughs required in order to move the business forward, and

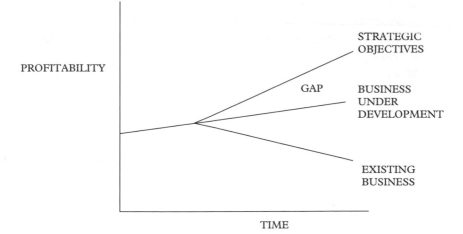

Fig. 4.1 Strategic gap analysis

- emphasizes the longer and medium term and is not just confined to the shorter term.

The cons of gap analysis are that it:

- is frequently used on its own – without supporting techniques, and
- typically results in superficial thinking, rather than in truly creative analysis of potential breakthroughs.

Gap analysis can be used for a wide number of applications, including:

- sales gaps – both short and medium term,
- profitability gaps – for three-year planning value gaps – for targeting shareholder value creation either at the corporate or business level,
- customer value gaps – the gap between what customers expect and what we deliver,
- competitor gaps – for understanding how we match up to our competitors,
- cost gaps – for targeting strategic cost reduction,
- competitor gaps – for understanding gaps in capability, and
- change gaps – for understanding the gap between where we are now in the change process and where we want to be in the future.

Killer takeaways from business planning are:

- Focus it principally in a small number of major breakthroughs (no more than three), and to a lesser extent on more minor areas of continuous improvement.
- Beware of using gap analysis when it's really CRAP analysis (creating artificial plans).
- Make sure that all your plans contain an element of cunning – otherwise why are you doing them?

Key links to other skills include:

- acquisitions (p. 15),
- alliances (p. 21),
- creativity (p. 245),
- financial planning (p. 154),
- imagination (p. 247),
- market development (p. 64),
- option generation (p. 249),
- product development (p. 69),
- report writing (p. 227),
- stakeholder management (p. 199), and
- summarizing (p. 202).

Reference

Ansoff, I. (1969) *Corporate Strategy,* Irwin, Homewood

CONTRACT MANAGEMENT

ontract management can be defined as: 'The commercial skills associated with agreeing a deal with either a buyer or supplier in order to gain advantages and sustainable terms.'

Contract management is an essential skill to have – even if you are not generally involved directly in a sales or buying function – as from time to time you are almost inevitably going to be involved in this area. Unless you have a reasonable level of skill, then it is very easy to submit to the demands of another party.

For example, a client of one of the authors (with whom a successful one-year relationship had been established) sent an e-mail with a very lengthy contract, without warning, on a Friday afternoon. The contract specified:

- €2 million commercial insurance,
- €1.2 million professional indemnity insurance,
- cancellation terms of 50% within 7 days, 25% within 14 days (his previous terms are 100% within two weeks, 75% within four weeks, 50% within six weeks), and
- guaranteed delivery of programmes at a level of '4' or 'good'.

This was obviously a case for Porter's five forces to come to the rescue – especially the relative bargaining power of the author relative to the client.

An e-mail was sent that weekend, which reminded the client that they appeared to be attempting to vary the contract, and it would be nice, if they did want to renegotiate any terms, to talk to the author personally.

Ultimately, some of these terms were just not acceptable, and might result in disruption to the relationship, if terms could not be agreed. Using storytelling, the client was persuaded to talk to the contracts department, and sort things out. Remaining cool in the face of such pressure is thus an essential skill for any manager and this requires a number of techniques:

- Porter's five forces (as illustrated in the example above).
- Option generation (think about what other options you/the other party have).
- Game theory (try to find a solution which means that both parties are better off, and no one is significantly worse off – relative to their expectations agendas).
- The out-of-body experience (imagine you are in their position).
- Storytelling (imagine how the negotiations *might* pan out, given your alternative negotiating strategies).

Killer takeaways from contract management:

- Determine your essentials and your tradeables.
- Redefine the situation if that is appropriate (for example, return to the time *before* someone moved the goalposts).
- Practise the art of the 'broken record' – keep going back to your original position, time and time again in negotiations.
- Don't make your arguments too complex, as they can sometimes then be more easily picked apart.
- Show them a way out – when there is an impasse.

Contract management is linked to other skills including:

- challenging (p. 243),
- influencing (p. 211),
- helicopter thinking (p. 40),
- negotiating (p. 92),
- option generation (p. 249),
- problem diagnosis (p. 254),
- risk and uncertainty analysis (p. 44), and
- storytelling (p. 47).

MARGIN MANAGEMENT

argin management can be defined as: 'The process of ensuring that one maximizes the value created (and captured) from a business activity, relative to the resources (and cost of resources) expended to achieve this.'

Margin management is thus about three key things:

- leverage – of value over cost,
- capture of value – through getting a fair proportion of value created then captured in your own price, and also in avoiding value destruction through any discounting, and
- avoiding wastage – deploying costs only in so far as they produce value (thus for example avoiding unsold stocks, rework, production errors or bottlenecks, or idle resources etc.).

The pros of margin management are that it:

- enhances shareholder value,
- avoids embarrassing drops in profitability, and
- ensures that there is always sufficient investment available for growth.

Margin management is needed both for new product launches/market entry, and also for continued protection and enhancement of one's existing business activities. Margin management needs to be adapted especially when one is moving through different phases of the product life cycle.

Relevant techniques for margin management are:

- Motivator/hygiene factors – to understand the basis of existing/new customer value creation.

- Porter's five forces – to understand shifts in industry dynamics and structure, and the resultant pressure on margins (e.g. new competitor entry, and the effect of substitutes).
- The negotiating techniques described in the section on 'Contract Management' (page 86).
- Storytelling/competitor analysis – especially in a bid context. What will competitors propose and how will they position their offering compared to yours? Is it advantageous to avoid being the cheapest bid (as this might signal dubious quality) and come in as the second cheapest, potentially?

Killer takeaways include:

- When pressed to take on business with a very low margin, extrapolate this to all your business: what would its profitability/rate of return be then, and would this be acceptable?
- When pressed to work under very difficult conditions (or for a very difficult customer) reflect on how awful this would be if *all* of your business was like this – should you be doing this?

Key links to other skills include:

- business planning (p. 82),
- contract management (p. 86),
- divestment (is it worthwhile getting out of some business areas?) (p. 28),
- market segmentation (is it even worthwhile being in this segment?) (p. 90),
- negotiating (p. 92), and
- strategic thinking (p. 49).

MARKET SEGMENTATION

Market segmentation is a key technique for developing effective marketing strategies and can be defined as: 'The process of separating out distinctive groups of buyers with similar needs and mindsets into manageable clusters – in order to develop more focused marketing strategies.'

Segmentation of buyers can be done for the business-to-business market at two levels: the company level (types of industry, size etc.) and also at the individual level (type of decision-maker, psychological type, etc.).

The pros of market segmentation include:

- more focused marketing strategies,
- more effective product development, promotions etc., and
- more effective organizational structures (especially for sales, service and distribution).

Whilst the textbooks (and marketing degree courses) often prescribe sophisticated approaches to market segmentation, the everyday management reality is very different. While segmentation exists in some organizations it is often very crude, to say the least. In financial services, for example, it is frequently limited to generic typologies of customers (characterized as different 'fruits' – oranges or apples etc. – to denote different styles of buying), rather than defined in a business-specific way.

We have (ourselves) a very clear idea of some of the micro-segments of our market, including:

- The 'adventurers' (those who want to try out new things in order to enhance their own organizational positions).
- The 'U-turners' (those who would like to be adventurers, but do quick U-turns at the first sign of any trouble).
- The 'conservationists' (those who are very wary of anything new and possibly destabilizing).
- The 'would-be consultants' (those who harbour real, or imagined ambitions to be consultants themselves, so they have secondary

agendas to learn from ourselves, which we actually do not have a problem with!).

The key point of segmentation is this: is it useful, and what value does it add? As in the above example, it can be most useful when adjusting one's behaviour in sales (or buying) – to reflect the style of the buyer.

A specific technique for segmenting the market is to take two dimensions and plot them against each other, as shown in the table below.

	Income levels			
Age group	Low	Medium	High	Very high
Children				
Teenagers				
Young adults				
Families – young children				
Families – teenagers				
Empty nesters				
Elderly				

For each one of these segments it is possible to do a motivator/hygiene factor analysis to characterize the distinctive turn-ons and turn-offs.

Killer takeaways on marketing segmentation include:

- What are you going to do with it anyway, once you have got it?
- Does your segmentation seem genuinely cunning – in any way?
- Which 20% of the market segments represent 80% of the value?

Key links to other techniques include:

- business planning (p. 82),
- customer awareness (p. 57),
- life-cycle management (p. 60),
- market development (p. 64),
- market research (p. 66),
- product development (p. 69), and
- selling (p. 72).

NEGOTIATING

 egotiating can be defined as: 'The process of agreeing a deal with another party which involves them feeling that they had actually got an acceptable deal, but one which is actually favourable to yourself.'

The pros of negotiating are that:

- it can give you an edge over the other party,
- it will help you to protect your margins, if it is effective, and
- it facilitates a key corporate ritual – unless you go through at least some of the motions, then the other party may feel unfulfilled.

The cons of negotiating are that:

- It can be very time consuming and frustrating.
- At the end of the day, it can be a negative-sum game: in a perfectly altruistic world no incremental value is created for both parties, so virtually all negotiating time and effort is technically value-destroying.
- If you drive too hard a bargain, then the deal may not be sustainable and, also, you might ultimately sell less.

Negotiating is needed in:

- buying situations,
- selling situations,
- buying/selling internal services – within organizations, and
- acquisitions, divestment and alliance deal-making.

Once again, the key techniques for negotiating were covered in 'Contract Management' (p. 86), and are to come in 'Stakeholder Management' (p. 199).

Killer takeaways in negotiation include:

- Always remember, 'I am not doing this to be liked'.
- If in doubt, defer any agreement. Buying time puts the other party in suspense, increasing their anxiety and perceived urgency to close a deal (unless they are under no particular time pressure).
- Always have great clarity about how relatively important the deal is to them/you. (Here you might also have to manage their perceptions downwards about how important it is to you, but without implying that you aren't prepared to be committed to deliver it.)

The key links to other skills include:

- contract management (p. 86),
- helicopter thinking (p. 40),
- influencing (p. 211),
- margin management (p. 88),
- market segmentation (p. 90),
- stakeholder management (p. 199),
- storytelling (p. 47), and
- value management (p. 165) – how much is the deal worth to them/to you, and who is capturing the most/least value?

PERFORMANCE ANALYSIS

P erformance analysis can be defined as: 'The systematic diagnosis of how a business, a department or an individual is performing – in terms of both performance drivers and brakes.'

Performance analysis is an essential skill for any general manger with profit responsibility. It is also important for financial managers, who still need to diagnose the performance of their support departments.

Performance analysis is needed:

- before the event – what will the key performance drivers be (in advance), for business planning purposes,
- during the event – to understand, and learn from current business performance, and to take immediate action (if appropriate/feasible), and
- after the event – for learning and feedback, and for input into new business plans.

A key technique for performance analysis (Grundy and Brown 2002) is that of key performance drivers.

Performance driver analysis helps to diagnose organizational performance, either externally or internally, or both. A second way of analysing business and financial performance is to identify the key performance drivers using a vector format.

Performance drivers here are drawn as vertical arrows and brakes are shown as downward arrows. Figure 4.2 illustrates this with reference to the perceived performance drivers of Rover cars, based on external data synthesized around late 1995. The length of these arrows determines their signifier, their relative importance.

Although this method does not purport to be an exact picture of Rover's performance drivers it does yield some important concerns about

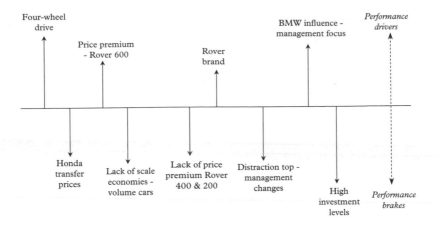

Fig. 4.2 Rover cars – performance

the medium-term attractiveness of BMW's acquisition of Rover, even if there were longer-term opportunities beyond this analysis.

Performance driver analysis can be used for:

- analysing a group's performance,
- understanding a business unit's performance,
- understanding a team's performance, and
- analysing an individual's performance.

Performance driver analysis is especially helpful in turnaround situations.

In many ways, performance driver analysis is more incisive than strengths and weaknesses, opportunities and threats (SWOT) analysis, as it focuses on those factors that have an impact on economic value generation in a business. This gets us away from the 'nice-to-haves', which often cloud up the 'strengths' of SWOT analysis. Also, with the vector format the performance drivers are automatically prioritized.

The pros of performance driver analysis are:

- the 'so-what?' drops out much more readily than in a SWOT analysis,
- it is already prioritized,
- it can be linked more closely to financial planning,

- it gives a better feel of the overall business context before addressing a specific business problem or bottleneck (so that we do not simply respond reactively to a problem),
- it makes judgements on performance less of a personal issue, and
- it can distinguish (in separate analysis) external and internal performance drivers.

In addition it may be useful to translate this analysis into a set of indicators, sometimes called KPIs or 'key performance indicators'. These list the measures/indicators against which success will be judged. So, for BMW's acquisition of Rover these might have been:

- Rover's unit costs are reduced by 20 per cent,
- successful integration of Rover's management – within 18 months,
- timely relaunch of the Mini (i.e. within three years),
- successful (and timely) launch of the Rover 75 (and related ranges) (within three years),
- eradication of quality problems with the Discovery four wheel drive (within two years),
- UK market share is protected, and
- exports are doubled.

In reality very few if any of these KPIs were ever realized.

A related approach is the balanced scorecard, which will be described in the later section 'Controlling' (p. 116).

Killer takeaways for performance drivers are:

- Ask: what is the one big thing you have forgotten? (In Rovers case the initial sterling exchange rate at the time of acquisition negotiations subsequently strengthened by 20%, impacting hugely on both sales volumes and margins.)
- Also ask: what is the second big thing you have forgotten? (Again, in Rover, investment levels had to be trebled to develop a truly competitive range of cars.)

Links to other skills now include:

- acquisitions integration (p. 107),
- business cases (p. 79),
- business planning (p. 82),
- divestment (p. 28),
- financial planning (p. 154),
- forecasting (p. 156),
- margin management (p. 88),
- option generation (p. 249),
- organizational design (p. 218) (for diagnosing organizational performance),
- problem diagnosis (p. 254),
- performance appraisal (p. 222),
- project appraisal (p. 98),
- storytelling (p. 47),
- targeting goals (p. 100),
- turnaround (p. 158), and
- understanding company accounts (p. 160).

References

Grundy, A.N. & Brown L. (2002) *Be Your Own Strategy Consultant*, Thomson Learning, London.

PROJECT APPRAISAL

Project appraisal is: 'The process of evaluating a project from a strategic, marketing, operational, financial and organizational prospective.'

The complete process of project appraisal is illustrated in Fig. 4.3 and it involves the following stages:

- Definition – scoping the project and defining its objectives.
- Options: exploring critical options for the decision and also any options that it forecloses.
- Targeting and data collection – targeting data after a first-cut review of the kind of external and internal assumptions which will need to be made about key value drivers.
- Assumptions – collecting and evaluating data through formulating the external and internal assumptions; then testing these assumptions, revisiting the key options, and working up contingency plans.
- Business case – preventing the business case and, where feasible, refining the programme to add more value at less cost and at lowest risk.
- Controls – translating the business case into monitoring measures and controls. (See Brown and Grundy 2002c for more.)

Project appraisal is an essential skill and only for the most obviously recognizable projects, but also for less obviously recognizable ones, like having a new member of staff, or taking a new job, etc. It is thus needed on an everyday basis.

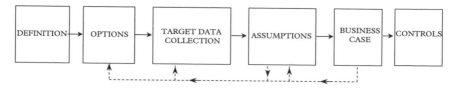

Fig. 4.3 Strategic project evaluation

One useful approach is therefore to identify the key issues (and/or objectives) that you face in your job and then to turn these into mini projects (with mini project plans). This can make you anything between 20 per cent and 50 per cent more effective – and allow you to scope work much earlier!

Relevant techniques include:

- Definition – fishbone analysis (see 'Problem Diagnosis', p. 254) or wishbone analysis (see 'Product Development', p. 69).
- Options – see the strategic option grid ('Option Generation', p. 249) and the cunning plan ('Strategic Thinking', p. 49).
- Target and data collection – the techniques in the strategy/marketing sections, and stakeholder analysis ('Stakeholder Management', p. 199).
- Assumptions – the uncertainty grid.
- Business case – see 'Business Cases', (p. 79).
- Controls – see fishbone analysis (in 'Problem Solving', p. 254) and the balanced scorecard ('Controlling', p. 116).

Killer takeaways include:

- Imagine this is not your project – what would you make of it then/or do if you were simply someone else?
- Is there a better project you could do, maybe *should* do?
- What new projects (which might be more attractive) might this one prevent you from doing?

Key linkages to other key skills include:

- business cases (p. 79),
- forecasting (p. 156),
- financial planning (p. 154),
- performance analysis (p. 94),
- problem diagnosis (p. 254),
- risk and uncertainty analysis (p. 44),
- stakeholder management (p. 199),
- storytelling (p. 47), and
- strategic thinking (p. 49).

Reference

Grundy, A.N. & Brown, L. (2002c) *Strategic Project Management*, Thomson Learning, London.

TARGETING GOALS

 argeting goals means defining the objectives that need to be delivered at the corporate, business, departmental, project and personal level.

The pros of targeting goals are:

- it gives greater clarity and focus to action,
- it can provide a consistent framework across the organization, and
- it can set priorities.

The cons of targeting goals are:

- there are frequently goals with no really viable action plans,
- the goals are often unrealistic,
- the goals can be inconsistent, or some goals dominate over this,
- the goals are sometimes changed producing cynicism,
- the goals are maintained, but assumed resources are reduced or removed, and
- delays occur but timelines are not adjusted.

Targeting goals thus seems to be a necessary evil in many organizations. This is a pity, as provided that they are managed in a common-sense way (conspicuously absent from many organizations) they can be fruitful.

Besides short-term goals, any business should focus on longer-term goals as well, otherwise the business may lose its sense of direction.

Goals are needed at:

- the corporate level,
- the business level,
- the functional level (marketing, operations, HR, finance, IT, etc.),
- the project level, and
- the level of the individual.

We have already covered some techniques for targeting goals, including:

- gap analysis, and
- key performance indicators.

We will go on to consider the relative balance of goals with the balanced scorecard – in 'Controlling' in Chapter 5.

A step-by-step process (using gap analysis) for targeting goals is:

1 Identify where you are now (A).
2 Identify where you really, really, really want to be (B).
3 Evaluate how effective existing plans or ideas might be to arrive at these goals (C) and what the remaining gap is (B–A–C).
4 Come up with your most cunning plan (Z) for how you might get there.
5 Revisit your gap analysis, and finalize your targeted goals, (G) (which is A + C + Z).

Killer takeaways for targeting goals are:

- Do not fill your gap with artificial plans (or 'CRAP' analysis).
- Remember that an average plan (that is, one with no real cunning associated with it) gives you no real competitive advantage

Targeting goals is linked to:

- action planning (p. 263),
- budgeting (p. 141),
- business planning (p. 82),
- controlling (p. 116),
- direction setting (p. 179),
- drive (p. 266),
- forecasting (p. 156),
- motivating (p. 192),
- policy setting (p. 194),
- prioritization (p. 277),
- proactivity (p. 281),
- stakeholder management (p. 199)(especially gaining ownership), and
- time management (p. 291).

TENDERING

Tendering is a most exciting pastime. Tendering involves managers bidding for work against other competitors.

The pros of tendering are that:

- it may get you large amounts of work, or work which may continue for a long time, and
- it shapes up your ability to compete.

The cons of tendering are that:

- it typically has a much worse set of five competitive forces (higher bargaining power of the buyers, growth rivalry, and potentially inferior margins (through more competitive prices), and
- it is potentially less financially attractive as you will only get, on average, a certain hit rate of sales through tendering – whilst the sales and management effort can be very expensive. (Interestingly, as a general policy – both of the authors do not engage in tendering, in their consultancy business – but see below for an exception!)

Tendering may be needed both to gain new work, and to retain existing work, but either way, more or less the same principles apply.

The relevant techniques that we have seen so far are:

- the out-of-body experience,
- motivator/hygiene factors, and
- wishbone analysis (see 'Product Development', p. 69).

We will add to that, stakeholder analysis (see 'Stakeholder Management, p. 199). Figure 4.4 below gives you a more detailed analysis of the out-of-body experience.

Tendering opportunities can also be evaluated by using expected value analysis. For instance, one of the authors was asked to bid for a

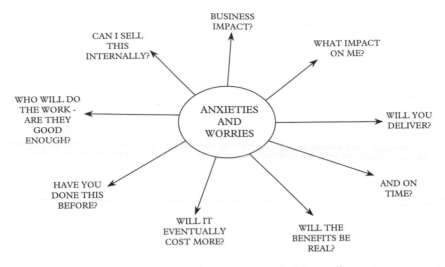

Fig. 4.4 Have the out-of-body experience – the decision maker

£10,000 contract against four other bidders. He was initially very reluctant to do this as the average expected value was:

One quarter or 25% × £10,000 = £2500; subtract the cost of his time to submit the tender and to do a presentation – £1000, leaving a net value of £1500 (a ratio of only 1.5 of incremental value against his initial investment cost).

The client was very keen nevertheless that they would like him to bid, and because of past contact with the client he believed he had a higher than average (or 35%) chance of being successful, other things being equal. He then decided to do two things. First he increased his proposed fees to £12,000, which would enable him to clear his break even value added more easily. He did not feel that the client would be particularly price sensitive, particularly as at least one of the bids would be from a larger organization, with a higher cost base (and thus higher pricing).

The second thing he did was to do an exceedingly thorough job on the proposal, focusing as much as possible on the added value to the client, and on a number of areas of competitive edge which would be very hard for other tenders to emulate. This took more time to propose, but he believed that the opposition would not be able to copy this, nor would wish to go as far as he was to secure the sale.

His revised expected value was then as follows:

Probability of winning the work　　= 45%
Cost of time　　　　　　　　　　= £1200
Fees (if successful)　　　　　　　= £12000
Expected pay-off　　　　　　　　= 45% × £12,000
　　　　　　　　　　　　　　　　　- £1200
　　　　　　　　　　　　　　　　= £4200

The leverage of expected pay-off over his bidding cost was now:

$$\frac{4200}{1200} = 3.5 \text{ (which was a considerable improvement)}$$

The bid strategy worked: he won the work and it was value generative!

Obviously, this bid might have gone the other way, but retrospective discussion with his new client suggested that his analysis had been fairly accurate.

Killer takeaways from tendering are thus:

- Avoid tendering if you can get business of equal quality (or nearly equal quality), elsewhere.
- Use expected values to test out your judgements, your strategy, if you can assign meaningful probabilities.
- If the expected value looks insufficient, just experiment to see if raising the price makes it worthwhile. You may decide it is then worth doing, where the situation is not necessarily highly price sensitive, or could be defined that way.

Linkages to other skills include:

- business users (p. 79) (for the client/customer),
- helicopter thinking (p. 40),
- negotiating (p. 92),
- questioning (p. 258) (the customer),
- risk and uncertainty analysis (p. 44),
- stakeholder management (p. 199) (within the customer), and
- storytelling (p. 47).

Operations Skills

ACQUISITION INTEGRATION

Acquisition integration brings us back to where we started – the consummation of the acquisition appraisal. Acquisition integration is defined as: 'The process of assimilating the activities of operations acquired in order to capture their economic value, and to develop them further.'

The integration phase is crucial as it is here that value is often diluted or destroyed rather than created. This may be due to a variety of reasons, for instance:

- New management might impose its own way of doing things and thus damage the acquisition's competitive strength. (At Rover Group, for example, BMW imposed its own notion of what 'Britishness' was about, mispositioning the brand.)
- There may be an abrupt change in management style, leading to lower morale and business performance rather than improved performance.
- Integration plans may be left to emerge and, if deliberate, are inadequately thought through to deal with obstacles to change.
- Alternatively, there may be no real change in the management at the top when one is badly needed, leading to drift (as at Rover during the first two years following acquisition).
- The acquisition period itself is a distracting time for incumbent management. There may be a period of months or longer when new developments are deferred, and during which costs are unwisely cut. During this period even the normal attention to customer delivery and retention may be lost.
- Key staff may leave, feeling (rightly or wrongly) that their career prospects are blunted.

The integration phase is crucial as it is during this period that the acquirer has most opportunity to learn from the acquisition. This learning should obviously deal with the post-acquisition performance of the acquisition – financially and strategically. But it should also cover the acquisition process itself.

We can now examine some useful techniques, firstly through fishbone analysis (see Fig. 5.1). Using the fishbone, the key symptom of the problem is shown at the right hand side of the page – at the fish's head. The underlying root causes of the problem are depicted as the bones of the fishbone.

Figure 5.1 highlights some of the main reasons for failure of acquisition integration. These reasons range from there not being an effective and robust strategy in the first place through to inadequate integration planning and project management and to inappropriate organizational change. Typically, unsuccessful integration is characterized by a lack of decisiveness on the part of the acquiring management team, or through inappropriate and damaging interventions in the acquired business.

It is useful also to examine (at a more positive level) what factors would need to line up to deliver a particularly effective implementation process. This is depicted in Fig. 5.2. Notice that while some of these alignment factors are reversals of the fishbone analysis, some of them are now, and all of them are not in any way average, but more superior or visionary.

Finally, organizational morale can easily go into a downward spiral during integration, especially where there are delays in agreeing new structures and roles. This can be represented in Fig. 5.3, where morale over time is plotted against organizational performance over time.

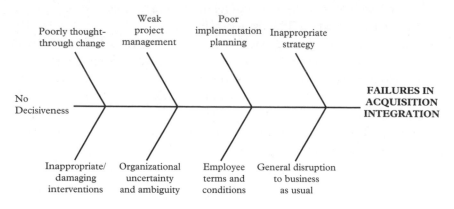

Fig. 5.1 A fishbone analysis of failures in acquisition integration

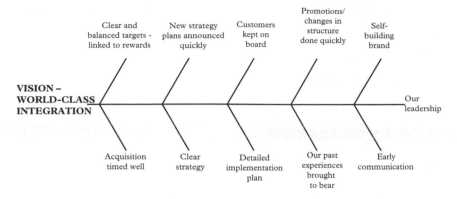

Fig. 5.2 A wishbone analysis of successes in acquisition integration

Killer takeaways from acquisition integration include:

- If you think you are going to need to make changes, do this as soon as possible – do not procrastinate.
- The decision as to what extent you do need to make changes depend very much on:
  - current management's strengths and weaknesses;
  - flexibility (or lack of it) of current management's mindset;
  - the requirements of the future business strategy and its associated competitive challenges;
  - the value which you feel you can add to the acquisition, and your own team's existing competencies; and

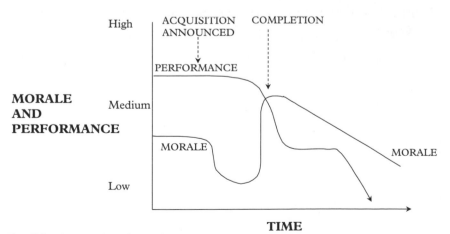

Fig. 5.3 Integration dynamics

- the amount of available management skills you have, and the opportunity cost of deploying them on this particular acquisition.

Acquisition integration is related to other key skills including:

- action planning (p. 263),
- business planning (p. 82),
- change management (p. 173),
- customer awareness (p. 57),
- controlling (p. 116),
- divestment (p. 28),
- energizing (p. 184),
- information collection (p. 120),
- listening (p. 190)(to the existing management and staff),
- motivating (p. 192),
- product development (p. 69),
- prioritization (p. 277),
- risk and uncertainty analysis (p. 44),
- resource management (p. 131),
- stakeholder management (p. 199),
- storytelling (p. 47),
- turnaround (p. 158) (potentially), and
- value management (p. 165).

Reference

Grundy, A.N. (2003) *Smart Things to Know About Acquisitions*, Capstone, Oxford.

BENCHMARKING

B enchmarking can be defined as: 'The data collection, analysis and learning from a variety of sources in order to identify how to compete and to perform more effectively.'

Benchmarking can help significantly to stretch your thinking about what is needed/possible – and thus to jolt you out of your current mindset. Equally, if there is *too much* of a focus on *measurement,* it can end up with just assessing how good you are against someone else. Benchmarking can be used for:

- business planning,
- input to strategy reviews,
- acquisition appraisal,
- cost management,
- organizational development,
- services strategy, and
- assessing management capability.

Benchmarking can take a variety of forms, including:

- Customer benchmarking – how well do you perform vis-à-vis customer perspectives? Use motivator/hygiene analysis for this.
- Competitor benchmarking – use the competitor profile technique for doing best-in-class benchmarking.
- Outsourcing benchmarking – are external suppliers better than your internal suppliers?

Best-in-class benchmarking can be done either outside your local market or in entirely different industries. The latter is particularly interesting, especially where other industries are more advanced, and where your existing competitors are very 'me-too'.

For instance, some years ago one of the authors introduced the Post Office to a security company (for a strategic lunch to discuss the business case for security investment). The Post Office learnt two things from this security company:

1   Define your benchmarking objective(s) and then think radically about options to achieve that objective(s) at the lowest cost (instead of defending their cost centres heavily, the security company simply hid the cash from prospective thieves!).
2   Instead of thinking about making an investment decision, just reduce the inherent (security) by cunning interview methods – the security company had learnt how to minimize the risk of having suspect staff.

This session was thus well worth the lunch – possibly saving millions of pounds.

A useful stage-by-stage process for benchmarking is:

- Define your own issues and objectives first (what do you want to learn, and why, and what might you do about it?).
- Perform the internal benchmarking: (how good/bad are you now, and why?).
- Select/approach benchmarking targets (prioritizing these carefully).
- External benchmarking – visits (to perhaps three to five companies).
- Distil the learning, involve stakeholders on the insights, and prioritize and plan your necessary follow-on action.

Killer takeaways from benchmarking include:

- Define the key questions you want to address up front.
- Before approaching benchmarking sites, imagine (psychically – as it were) what you might be able to learn.
- Be open – share your learnings with the site.
- Reflect *as soon as* you have done the visit – whether this is in a pub, in a Little Chef, or even in the car park.
- Involve key stakeholders who will be involved in any subsequent change-in the visits to other companies (to build their ownership).
- Project manage the entire process skilfully.

Benchmarking has close relationships with other skills, including:

- acquisitions appraisal (p. 15) (especially company and competitor benchmarking),
- buying (p. 114) (for outsourcing),
- change management (p. 173),
- competitor awareness (p. 25) (competitor profiling),
- customer awareness (p. 57) (motivator/hygiene factors),
- global awareness (p. 38) (world-class benchmarking),
- listening (p. 190) (which is an absolutely key skill within the process),
- negotiating (p. 92) (access – to sites),
- option generation (p. 249) (with whom to benchmark and how),
- organization and people planning (p. 220) (as external analysis),
- outsourcing (p. 126),
- product development (p. 69),
- questioning (p. 258) (as part of the process),
- report writing (p. 227),
- stakeholder management (p. 199),
- strategic thinking (p. 49), and
- storytelling (p. 47).

BUYING

uying is an important skill, even if you are not a buyer. Buying is the process of getting the best mix of value, cost, quality and risk – whether from external, or internal sources. (Even if you are not paying for it with hard cash, purchasing an internal product or service is also buying.)

The relevant techniques/skills for effective buying include:

- Porter's five forces (see 'Economic Awareness (Micro)', p. 33 for managing, and potentially optimizing your bargaining power, and managing rivalry).
- The strategic option grid (see 'Option Generation', p. 249 – for evaluating different buying routes).

A process for buying can be defined as:

- Defining 'what you really, really, really want' – your objective.
- Exploring the external and internal options (of supply sources) – from whom to buy.
- Collecting data about these sources of supply, trading off their:
  - value,
  - cost,
  - quality, and
  - risk.
- Evaluating this data.
- Making the buying decision.
- Monitoring, control, and renegotiating.

Data on buyer sources can be drawn from:

- the supplier direct,
- from other customers, and
- from their annual report and accounts/other financial sources.

This data needs to be skilfully integrated – including observing the general behaviour of the supplier. For example one major bank hired a software company to implement a major IT project. After some months one of the bank's managers visited the supplier. Going into the kitchen she noticed a sign saying 'Please Bring Your Own Tea Bags'. (These had been provided for staff by the company previously.) She thought, 'I wonder if they are going bust?' They did, just one month later, leaving the bank with a huge problem.

Some killer takeaways on buying are:

- Make sure you have a strong relationship with one key contact at the supplier who is a) competent to fix things; b) on your own wavelength; and c) someone who you can always gain quick access to.
- Ensure that they are really focused on quality and that they are made aware that persistent non-delivery of pre-agreed service standards will mean a loss of business – but at the same time avoiding so much pressure that they can't handle it.
- Always try to have some other options up your sleeve (especially for other sources of supply). But be as open with them about your buying strategy and tactics as you can, to improve co-operation longer term.

The above points represent a tough balancing act to achieve.

Buying is associated with many other key skills, including:

- contract management (p. 86),
- controlling (p. 116),
- cost management (p. 146),
- motivation (p. 192),
- negotiating (p. 92),
- option generation (p. 249),
- outsourcing (p. 126),
- proactivity (p. 281),
- problem diagnosis (p. 254),
- strategic thinking (p. 49) (about supply sources), and
- teamworking (p. 229) (with the supplier).

CONTROLLING

C ontrolling is a skill without which you may well limit your career at some point in the future.

Controlling means: 'Being continually aware of how you are performing, and why you are performing that way.'

Controlling is needed for:

- monitoring ongoing business performance,
- developing new businesses,
- acquisition integration, and
- project management.

Over-controlling, however, can be a very bad idea as you can spend nearly all of your time monitoring performance rather than actually doing things, or thinking ahead. Over-control can also stultify others, and demotivate them.

One example of over-control was at Champney's Health resort when the new general manager arrived some years ago during its turnaround. He was quoted as saying when showing the cleaners around, 'This bit is actually not dirty. It isn't *actually dirty at all*, but it is just one of the things that you have to do. Do you get it? Are we now on the same wavelength?'

Key techniques for controlling include:

- performance driver analysis (already covered),
- fishbone analysis (see 'Problem Diagnosis', p. 254),
- the importance/influence grid (see Fig. 5.4),
- key performance indicators (see 'Performance Analysis', p. 94), and
- the balanced scorecard.

Importance and influence analysis helps us to look at the extent to which we have control over various strategic factors, or we do not have control over them (see Fig. 5.4).

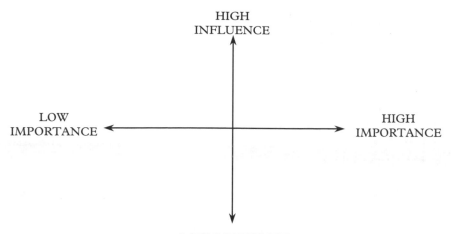

Fig. 5.4 The importance/influence grid

Most attention is often drawn to those areas which we have most influence over – and which are the most important – rather than those which are both *most important* and where we have *least influence* (the southeast of the importance/influence grid).

Yet it is frequently possible – through being creative – to gain at least some influence over these areas.

Importance/influence analysis can be used:

- as part of a scenario development process,
- when influencing stakeholders: to determine where the pivotal points of influence might be, and
- to challenge one's own mindset that some things are simply beyond one's control.

The pros of importance/influence analysis are that it:

- encourages managers to think more proactively about what they can do about issues, rather than just monitoring for its own sake, and
- helps them to scan their own external and internal environment and also acts as prompts for action.

The balanced scorecard is another technique which can be deployed both to broaden and counterbalance your scope of control. In its original formulation (Kaplan and Norton), it specified four key areas of control:

- customer satisfaction,
- operational efficiency,
- organizational morale, and
- financial performance.

The original objective of this technique was to help managers avoid overdependency on monitoring financial measures. Whilst being highly plausible in theory, the balanced scorecard has a number of potential drawbacks as follows:

- Its title suggests that it is a trendy management, which implies that it is unlikely to be sustainable.
- It can be so counter culture that senior managers will never take it really seriously.
- It can very easily become overcomplex and unwieldy.
- It might be inefficient and ineffective unless it is tailored to the industry and organizational context.
- It is often implemented without revisiting the format and content of the strategy, and without appropriate links to rewards systems, or without sufficient training, appropriate information systems, or positioning generating.

In addition, there is a not-so-straightforward relationship between organizational morale and business performance generally. Personally, if anything, we prefer this fourth category to be 'innovation and development'.

Killer takeaways on the balanced scorecard are:

- Tailor it to your own business context.
- Devise a maximum of five macro areas of monitoring, and for each of these add an additional five – more micro – and specific areas for establishing indicators/measures. This could include, for example, financial performance – free cash flow; or for innovation and development – the percentage of business due to innovation and development over the last two years.
- Don't focus equally and simultaneously on all measures – choose three key areas per month/quarter to target breakthrough improvements in – rather than spreading yourself across all (maximum) twenty-five. Once a particular performance issue is fixed, move on to others.
- Make it positive and exciting, otherwise it becomes the 'balanced scared card'!

- Consider adapting the five categories of the strategic option grid as more relevant measures and ones which are more likely to map onto the strategy (see the section on 'Option Generation' p. 249).

Links to other skills include:

- acquisition integration (p. 107),
- business planning (p. 82),
- financial planning (p. 154),
- performance analysis (p. 94),
- prioritization (p. 277),
- performance analysis (p. 94),
- policy setting (p. 194),
- problem diagnosis (p. 254), and
- targeting goals (p. 100).

References

Kaplan, R.S. & Norton, D.P. 'The Balanced Scorecard – Measures that Drive Performance', *Harvard Business Review*, January–February, 1992.

INFORMATION COLLECTION

I nformation collection is something which many managers are not
so good at. They collect too little information, too much, or the
wrong information. And when they collect it, they often misinter-
pret it, too.

Information collection is the ability to gain maximum insights out
of the available data and in the most cunning and effective way possible.
Information collection is required to exercise a multitude of our skills,
and can be done both formally, or informally. Its pros are that:

- decisions can be made on more solid evidence,
- arguments about otherwise subjective matters can be resolved,
  and
- judgements can be more openly challenged.

A useful process for information collection is to ask:

- What are we trying to achieve, anyway?
- What value will collating data bring to this issue?
- What are our options for collecting data and by whom?
- What is our cunning plan – both for collecting and interpreting it?
- How can we achieve this with least time, cost, difficulty and disrup-
  tion?
- What key questions should we now formally set – to focus our inves-
  tigations?

A wonderful technique for focusing data collection is the uncertainty/
importance grid (which we saw in 'Risk and Uncertainty Analysis', p. 44).
Here we focus our data collection on those areas which are both:

- very uncertain, and
- very important.

A further technique where there are a range of potential options to be investigated is the strategic option grid (see 'Option Generation' p. 249). Here, we focus the data collection on those boxes which we consider to be a) most important and b) most uncertain about. For instance, we might find the option box of 'uncertainty and risk' to be both a) something very important and b) something we are very unsure about.

Killer takeaways here include:

- Never collect data unless you know what you are going to do with it.
- Collect only so much data that you can manage to interpret it.
- Don't collect anything if you can't do some storytelling (in advance) about its possible value.
- Treat the exercise as if it were a consulting project – how much would it cost at a notional day rate, times the time actually spent, and would that cost be worth it?
- The Internet is not the answer to everything in the world of data collection.

Links to other skills include:

- all strategy development skills (p. 13ff),
- business cases (p. 79),
- business planning (p. 82),
- buying (p. 114),
- financial planning (p. 154),
- forecasting (p. 156),
- market development (p. 64),
- outsourcing (p. 126) (of data collection),
- performance analysis (p. 94),
- problem diagnosis (p. 254),
- product development (p. 69),
- project appraisal (p. 98),
- questioning (p. 258),
- recruiting (p. 225),
- report writing (p. 227), and
- summarizing (p. 202).

IT AWARENESS

I T awareness can be defined as: 'Being able to use the more basic IT skills (e-mail, Internet, spreadsheets, databases etc.) adequately, and also, knowing how IT can be used to increase value added to the business, or deliver value in new ways, or help to reduce costs.'

The pros of IT are that:

- it can revolutionize your business model – through delivering value to customers in new ways,
- it can accelerate decision-making considerably, and
- it can be a vehicle for knowledge management – or the systematic use of knowledge to add value to the business.

But one con is that it can generate a lot of waste – through a high proportion of time being spent by managers on the computer, which is hardly value creating, and potentially value diluting or destroying.

A technique used to prioritize IT strategy found invaluable in the past is the attractiveness/implementation difficulty (AID) analysis which we see below (Fig. 5.5).

Beginning with the vertical dimension of attractiveness (on the AID grid or benefits costs), one can now expand on the final bullet point above.

It is sometimes the case that some parts of a possible IT strategy can be undertaken without doing others. Even where an IT strategy consists of a number of discretionary sub-parts or projects, which are not discretionary, it is still possible to display their individual positionings on the AID grid. Without doubt some parts of the IT strategy will be more difficult to implement than others, and will also contribute more to attractiveness – and will thus have different positionings on the AID grid.

Thinking now about the vertical dimension of attractiveness, each part of an IT strategy may vary in its relative benefits, and in its relative cost.

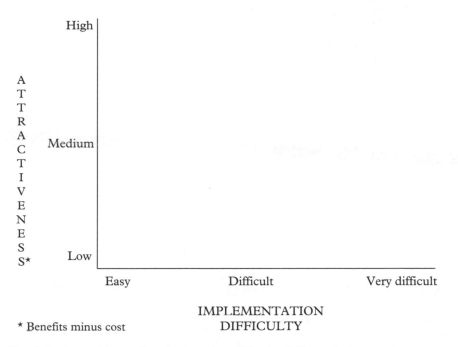

Fig. 5.5 Attractiveness/implementation difficulty (AID) analysis

The AID grid thus enables trade-offs to be achieved between strategies. The vertical dimension of the picture focuses on benefits less costs. The horizontal dimension represents the total difficulty over time. This time is defined as being the total time up until delivery of results, and not just to the completion of earlier IT project phases. This tool therefore enables a portfolio of possible projects to be prioritized, with Fig. 5.6 illustrating a hypothetical case.

IT Strategy A is seen as being both very attractive and relatively easy to implement. This project is non-contentious and will probably be given the go-ahead. IT Strategy C is relatively difficult – it will probably end up being zapped unless it can be reformulated to make it both a lot more attractive and easier.

To summarize, AID analysis can be used:

- to prioritize breakthroughs as a portfolio,
- to evaluate business plans,
- to evaluate the sub-components of a particular breakthrough, or project, and
- to track (in real time) a specific area of strategy implementation.

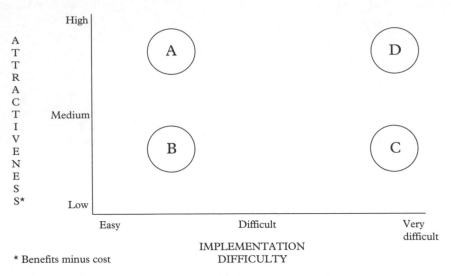

Fig. 5.6 Attractiveness/implementation difficulty (AID) analysis – example

The pros of AID analysis are that it is a:

- quick and easy technique to use, and
- visual way of representing and debating priorities.

Its potential cons are that:

- It can be subjective, unless it is accompanied by further analysis – for example of value and cost drivers for attractiveness (see 'Cost Management', p. 146) or of forcefield analysis (for implementation difficulty – see 'Change Management', p. 173).
- It can just represent existing thinking on a specific breakthrough, rather than more creatively defining the cunning plan.

Killer takeaways on IT awareness are:

- If your IT department can't ever seem to deliver anything – consider threatening to outsource all, or part of it.
- Use the strategic option grid (see 'Option Generation' p. 249) for any complex IT issues, including possible outsourcing.

Key linkage to other skills include:

- business cases (p. 79) (for appraising IT projects),
- change management (p. 173) (for implementing IT),
- controlling (p. 116) (finding better ways of monitoring your business),
- market development (p. 64) (for finding new IT-based distribution routes to market),
- problem diagnosis (p. 254) (use fishbone analysis for helping you to work out why your computer isn't working!),
- strategic thinking (p. 49) (for helping set your IT strategy), and
- time management (p. 291) (for making this *more* effective, and *not* *less*).

OUTSOURCING

O utsourcing can be defined as: 'The process of selecting, evaluating and managing outside suppliers – in order to leverage
their competitive advantage, and value added.' Outsourcing is
perhaps most applicable to those competencies which are less
at the heart of your own organization – especially those concerned with
the delivery of distinctive value to customers.

The pros of outsourcing are that it can:

- potentially reduce costs,
- simplify existing operations, making it easier to generate future
  growth – spared of the distraction of sourcing peripheral value
  – creating activities from within, and
- produce better quality, in which the outsourced supplier may become
  focused far more (contractually) on delivering targeted results than
  someone internally.

The potential cons of outsourcing, however, include:

- it can be difficult to both choose and manage the outsourced supplier (this needs new skills in its own right), and
- whilst your outsourced costs might be lower, their quality can be
  lower too, resulting in an overall loss of profitability, or damage
  indirectly to the company's brand.

Key techniques in outsourcing which we have covered/are covering
elsewhere:

- Fishbone analysis (see 'Problem Diagnosis', p. 254) – why do we
  perceive that there is a need to outsource?
- Motivator/hygiene factors.
- The strategic option grid (see 'Option Generation', p. 249).

The strategic option grid is particularly helpful in this specific situation. To perform an appraisal of suppliers you can use the generic criteria (used elsewhere in this book) of:

- strategic attractiveness,
- financial attractiveness,
- implementation difficulty,
- stakeholder acceptability, and
- risk and uncertainty.

Alternatively, you might set more tailored criteria to meet your more specific requirements, for example:

- cost reduction,
- ease of management,
- error-free delivery,
- qualitative factors,
- supplier response times, and
- security of supply.

Obviously, any outsourcing needs to be accompanied by a formal business case. To compile such a case properly it is important that you remember to compare performance levels associated with:

1 the current in-house situation,
2 outsourced options, and
3 the in-house situation now managed a quantum better (for example with different processes, staff, skill, structure etc.).

Killer takeaways for outsourcing thus include:

- Have 'strategic amnesia' – forget about who/how your current services are delivered, then look at the options for delivery of them, relative to 'what you really, really want', from scratch.
- Think about what provision you will need in two or even three or more years time, rather than just now – will this outsourced supplier is a sustainable relationship?
- Benchmark against other companies who have outsourced similar functions to yours – did this actually work, and what were the learning lessons, particularly for its implementation?

Outsourcing is linked to a number of skills, including:

- benchmarking (p. 111),
- business cases (p. 79),
- controlling (p. 116),
- cost management (p. 146),
- negotiating (p. 92),
- option generation (p. 249),
- storytelling (p. 47), and
- strategic thinking (p. 49).

PROCESS MANAGEMENT

P rocess management is defined as being: 'The skill of designing and/or implementing business and management processes, either at a tactical, or strategic level.'

Process management is relevant to a wide variety of operations, including:

- financial systems,
- information systems,
- purchasing,
- manufacturing,
- distribution, and
- servicing.

But in addition to that, processes can be devised for cross-functional processes, including:

- strategic decision-making,
- managing acquisition,
- divestment,
- product/market development,
- turnaround,
- people and capability development, and
- project management.

These are much more focused at a management level.

The essence of process management is continued in five key steps, namely:

- defining the outputs, then
- defining the steps which need to be carried out to produce these outputs, and then
- defining these inputs,

- defining the resources: people, skills, IT, and
- ensuring that the resulting process is as simple and as easy as possible to implement, reduces errors and cost, and also maximizes the value of its outputs.

We have seen some high-level processes defined for example in the sections on:

- acquisitions, and
- change management.

Besides these process pictures (which are relatively simple, and are linear in form), more sophisticated pictures can be drawn with process flow diagrams with all kinds of loops. Unfortunately, the pictures can get highly complex, and virtually unintelligible.

One of the authors saw a massive picture of the above kind at a leading software company, which was almost the size of an entire office wall – like a mural. Ironically, it was for project management – the very course which he was teaching them at the time. Once again, beware complexity indulged in for its own sake.

Killer takeaways include:

- To be a truly successful manager, it is often more crucial to define the management process than to get stuck into the detailed issues themselves.
- Always ask – what is the intended value of the process? (Rather than get tempted into intoxicating detail and complexity.)

Process management relates to a number of other key skills, including:

- problem-solving, and
- re-engineering.

It is required for many, if not most, of the one hundred business skills contained in this book.

RESOURCE MANAGEMENT

R esource management is about managing all resources within your organization – in order to maximize the present and future value of that resource. Resource management is thus not just about manager costs, but is also about leveraging value in relation to cost. Resource management is also applicable to not only business units costs but corporate head office costs, and can be applied to the departmental, project or even individual level.

Resource management (if pursued as above) will help not only to improve financial results, but is also a key vehicle of achieving a sustainable competitive advantage. In fact it is at the heart of one important strategy theory: resource-based competitive advantage (Grant 1991), which suggests that having access to distinctive/scarce resources is a major ingredient of competitive advantage.

Useful techniques for managing the resource base include value and cost drivers. A value driver is defined as 'any factor, both within or outside the business which is likely to generate cash inflows, either now or in the future, either directly or indirectly'. A cost driver is defined as 'any factor, both within or outside the business which is likely to generate cash outflows, either now or in the future, either directly or indirectly.'

A more general example of a value driver is 'customer attrition', whilst that of a cost driver in the banking industry is 'the number of bank branches managed by a senior bank manager' or 'the amount of time that we spend in meetings'.

Value- and cost-driver analysis can be used to restructure a company's resource base in order to avoid resources (and costs) being managed primarily on a short-term basis, and in isolation.

Figures 5.7 and 5.8, which depict a value- and cost-driver analysis for supermarket trolleys, give us an excellent example of these concepts. Here we see the value drivers being split down into 'value to the customer' and 'company value' – to give the macro-level value drivers for a new type of supermarket trolley. The macro cost drivers have a different split, these being analysed over the new supermarket trolleys' life cycle of costs. Alternative ways of analysing the cost breakdown are:

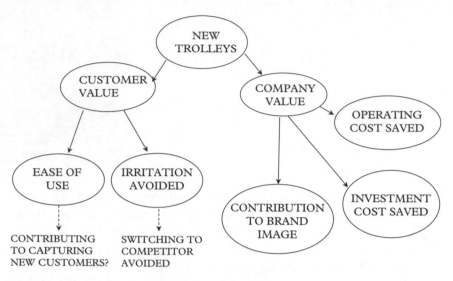

Fig. 5.7 Value drivers – new supermarket trolleys

- cost by activity,
- cost by process, and
- cost through the transaction cycle.

Most managers using value- and cost-driver analysis for the first time tend to copy relatively slavishly whatever example is given to them (like the above example of an innovative supermarket trolley). Whilst this usu-

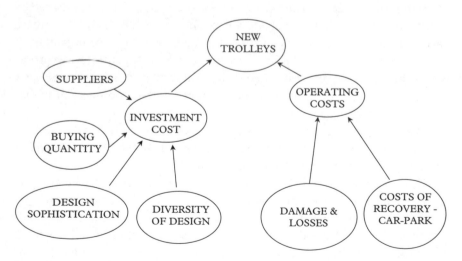

Fig. 5.8 Cost drivers – new supermarket trolleys

ally comes off, it is important to realize that the structure of value and cost drivers will vary according to the specific situation.

To illustrate this let us look at a second example. In Figs 5.9 and 5.10 we see the value and cost drivers of our (small) consultancy potentially investing in a Web site. We were sceptical as to its potential value (at that time) not only in terms of 'will we get more business?' but also 'will it be the quality we are targeting?'. Also, being very busy already, the obvious point was how we would accommodate much more work.

This particular value- and cost-driver analysis for our own business was done in around six minutes in a café in Edinburgh, overlooking the castle. Tea and croissants were consumed simultaneously, highlighting the fact that these analyses can be done very, very quickly.

The figures were illuminating. The key insights (which were not there before) were that:

- More value was likely to be added (at least in the medium term) from selling more to existing clients (for instance by encouraging them to look at our Web site), rather than by hits to the Web site from potential new clients.
- New hits might come from companies which were geographically distant (like South Africa, or Tibet), costing more in travel time and inconvenience to service.
- The costs of maintaining the Web site could easily exceed set-up costs, as would the cost of our time to input into the design of the site.
- There were considerable downside costs through competitors surveying our Web site, seeking to copy our products.

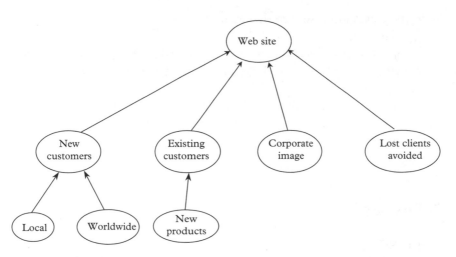

Fig. 5.9 Value drivers – Web site

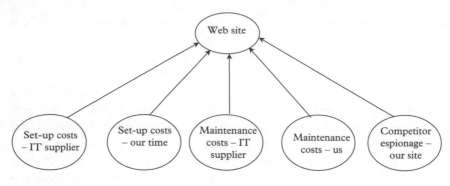

Fig. 5.10 Cost drivers – Web site

- The protective value of the Web site was intriguing. If one did not have a Web site how would one track lost business to competitors *with* Web sites?

So, value and cost drivers can be most fruitful ways of managing resources for competitive advantage (besides their use in cost management). These tools can be used also for analysing and evaluating:

- acquisitions (p. 18),
- business cases (p. 79),
- outsourcing (p. 126),
- process management (p. 129),
- product development (p. 69), and
- project appraisal (p. 98).

Killer takeaways in resource management are:

- Apply the 'zero-based' test – if you started again with no resources, what resource base would you now wish to acquire, bearing in mind the future?
- Help to improve flexibility of resources by adopting a 'robbing Peter to pay Paul' policy – tell people that they need to stop doing things of lesser value (with resources), so that they can spend more time doing more valuable things with them.

Reference

Grant, R.M., 'The Resource-Based Theory of Competitive Advantage: Implications for Strategy Formulation', (Spring 1991), *California Management Review*, pp 114–135.

TECHNOLOGY AWARENESS

T echnology awareness is crucial because technology can transform your business model. Technology can be defined as: 'A physical way of achieving either higher value output or more output, and potentially at a lower cost.'

Information technology is ultimately based on physical technologies, even if we can see them (as they are electronic, tiny currents on a microchip). Even in the authors' lifetimes, technology has transformed our business lives.

The pros of technology awareness are that it:

- opens your mind to what may be possible, and
- might give you a major advantage over your competitors

But a con is that you sometimes get intoxicated with a technology idea, without realizing that a large number of alignment factors, both within or outside your control, are required for it to create real value.

Technology awareness is very much about thinking about, and especially competing for, the future (Hamel and Prahalad 1994). This involves anticipating futures, which requires imagination, storytelling, and scenario building.

For instance, one of the authors consulted for a major supermarket chain in the mid-1990s – to develop home shopping.

Technology-wise, this required:

- information systems to manage orders and deliveries, and
- customers to be on the Internet in sufficient numbers to make it economically viable.

But the one big thing that seemed to have been missed (by the supermarket chain) was the electronically based picking systems that had to be in place in order to do the picking activity both to high quality standards and to low unit costs.

Unfortunately, it would seem that centralized picking systems have not been implemented generally within the industry, meaning that home shopping requires costly replication of effort: the customers still have to choose (go on the Internet etc.), and someone else (who is now paid) physically sorts the order. So, overall, apart from the rich and those who hate driving cars around themselves, the world is little better off – in terms of welfare and value.

Technology take-off (as the above example on home shopping in the supermarket industry highlights), usually occurs where the technology:

- reduces costs by a quantum amount, or
- where it gives a huge psychological turn-on to the customer, or
- where it allows an existing or new competitor to use it to gain market dominance, or
- where it allows major replication – possibly free of charge, or for minimal cost (like copying CDs, or software or other media etc.).

An example of a new technology where the jury is still out (as of 2003) is picture messaging for mobiles. Apart from the trendy, youth market, it is not easy to find a real use for it – except, perhaps, in the most unlikely situations.

For example, one of the authors woke up and looked outside the front window of his home to find several stray horses treading deep hoof prints in his front lawn, grazing on the grass and some of his small shrubs. They appeared to have escaped from a nearby field, previously put there by gypsies. Besides the obvious lawn damage there were problems, as motorists were swerving to avoid them in the road.

He thought, 'if only I had picture messaging – I could have e-mailed a photo to the local newspaper and to the police – who said on the telephone that they weren't interested, and were too busy anyway, presumably catching motorists doing 34 miles per hour.'

So at last I had found a potential use for a £400 phone costing £80 a month, which would otherwise seem exorbitant.

But, returning to our main story, and to summarize, our key techniques for technology appraisal are:

- AID analysis – how attractive/difficult would it be for customers (broken down by market segment) to use a particular new technology (like mobile telephone picture messaging)?
- Motivator/hygiene factors – what does the technology do in terms of value added/destroyed?

- Value and cost drivers – what might a business case look like to invest in it?
- Wishbone analysis, scenarios and the uncertainty grid – what would have to line up to deliver this future state of the world?

Killer takeaways on technology awareness include:

- What key habits, behaviours and mindsets would have to change for a new technology to really catch on?
- What key 'transitional events' would initiate lift-off of the new technology (for example, for a takeoff in grocery home shopping to occur, the price of a PC might need to drop to £600/and Internet usage using above, covering say 30 per cent of the population).
- In the longer term, what kind of company is likely to have a sustainable competitive position in the market, and with what competencies and mindset for the new technology?

Technology awareness is related to:

- competitor awareness (p. 25),
- cost management (p. 146),
- customer awareness (p. 57),
- global awareness (p. 38),
- market awareness (p. 62),
- product development (p. 69),
- resource management (p. 131),
- storytelling (p. 47),
- strategic thinking (p. 49), and
- uncertainty and risk analysis (p. 44).

Reference

Hamel, G. & Prahalad, C.K. (1994) *Competing for the Future*, Harvard Business School Press, MA.

Finance Skills

BUDGETING

udgeting is defined as: 'The short-term planning of resources and of costs to meet the profitability goals of the company.'

Budgeting, whilst focusing a great deal on financial data, also sets down the pattern of resource allocation both within a part of, and across, a company's operations.

There are a number of different types of budgets, including:

- sales budgets,
- cost budgets,
- capital budgets, and
- manpower budgets.

The pros of budgets are that:

- Without them managers could easily spend either too much, or underspend (as they do not feel they have sufficient authority to commit funds).
- They help to ensure that profitability goals are delivered, for example through highlighting a gap between sales performance and budget.

The cons of budgets are that:

- they are often very time consuming to prepare,
- they are frequently highly political,
- they are often created in such a way as to be inconsistent with the delivery of the longer-term strategy,
- they are often inflexible, and
- where they are changed, it is usually downwards, in terms of budgeted costs – when sales are less than anticipated, costs are cut, undermining inappropriately both short-term operational delivery and future strategy development.

Typically a budget will be developed with its 'hard' elements (set with tight targets) and with also some 'soft' elements such as the training or travel budgets. The softer elements are then manipulated by senior management in order to a) pay for either unexpected cost/overruns or b) sales shortfalls – in order to sustain budgeted levels of profitability. The training budget, in particular, is often used for unexpected, one-off consultancy needs.

Techniques for managing budgets much more effectively include:

- Motivator/hygiene factor and competitor profiling analysis – this can be used to highlight the specific resource deficiencies and blockages which are causing key competitive weaknesses, and adverse performance.
- Compiling business cases for major areas of revenue spend.
- Value and cost drivers – for trading-off value against costs.
- 'AID' analysis for budget prioritization.
- The balanced scorecard – for helping to avoid too much of a focus on financial results, to the detriment of other, non-financial goals.

Budgeting relates to a number of key skills areas, including:

- business planning (p. 82),
- controlling (p. 116),
- cost management (p. 146),
- financial planning (p. 154),
- forecasting (p. 156),
- information collection (p. 120),
- performance analysis (p. 94),
- prioritization (p. 277), and
- value management (p. 165).

CASH-FLOW MANAGEMENT

I n any difficult trading environment, cash flow is king! When times are easier, companies tend to forget about the importance of cash flow. History is littered with high-growth companies who get overly creative with their accounting – like Enron – and then find that whilst they can manipulate accounting profit, they cannot so easily manipulate cash.

Ultimately, net cash flow is a more effective and economic means of evaluating company performance, not accounting profit measures, which are distorted by accounting adjustments and conventions. Indeed, some corporations (like BP and Lloyds Bank) now prefer to target and manage their 'free cash flow'. This is operating profit with depreciation added back, less the cash required to invest in the business to sustain it at its current cash-generation capacity.

Cash-flow management is now defined as being: 'The process of planning, forecasting and controlling long-term cash flows in order to keep the company healthy, to satisfy its shareholders, and to meet its liabilities without significant risk of going bust.'

Cash-flow management thus requires:

- credit control,
- policies for paying suppliers,
- stock control, and
- control over capital (and other investment, including acquisitions).

These are, essentially, the management of any areas where there is a time lag between incurring a liability and the cash settlement of that liability.

A secondary function of cash-flow management is that of managing the cash once you have collected it, or treasury management (to earn interest or to protect against incurring foreign exchange or other losses etc.).

The pros of cash-flow management are thus:

- it preserves trading capability – in difficult terms, and
- it ensures that strategies can still be developed.

Besides the management of ongoing business – cash-flow management is even more crucial during turnarounds, where inattention to cash flow can trigger the company going under.

Key techniques for cash-flow management include:

- In the company's funds-flow statement (see the annual report and accounts), calculate the ratio of internal versus external sources of funds (if external sources of finance are a very high proportion of total funds – say over 70 per cent, this can signal difficulties – see Grundy 1998).
- Also the company's cash-flow statement should be able to give you (approximately) the company's free cash flow (or operating profits, added back depreciation, less sustainable investment levels). How much is the free cash flow relative, to net assets, and is this ratio increasing/reducing? (Albeit crude, this gives you a feel of value creation relative to the resource base.)
- Remaining balance sheet ratios like:
  - the number of days sales tied up in stocks (over 60 days is normally very bad news),
  - the number of days of purchases represented by trade creditors (if this is over 90 days it can suggest the company is about to go bust, as suppliers will press very hard for payment after this),
  - the number of days' cost of sales represented by stocks (depending on the industry, over 60 days can be unhealthy), and
  - liquidity ratios – the ratio of liquid assets (excluding stocks but including debtors) relative to liquid liabilities. (If this is much less than a ratio of one, the company may be on the brink of insolvency.)
- Are there any dubious looking contingent liabilities (in the notes to the accounts)?

Killer takeaways include:

- Get rid of all unnecessary delays in turning sales into cash, for example:
  - always bill work-in-progress each month, and
  - send invoices out when deliveries are made, and not at the end of the month.

- Do not tolerate debtors paying in 60 days when your payment terms are, say, 30. Chase them the very first day when they are overdue – get your debtors trained to pay on time!
- Don't annoy your suppliers unnecessarily by dragging out payment beyond their terms – as it undermines their commitment to deliver quality to you. You will pay for this in other ways, almost certainly, through their reduced loyalty and ultimately, performance.

Cash-flow management is thus related to:

- budgeting (p. 141),
- controlling (p. 116),
- credit control (p. 149),
- forecasting (p. 156),
- project appraisal (p. 98),
- selling (p. 72) (especially in credit control), and
- turnaround (p. 158).

Reference

Grundy, A.N. (1998) *Exploring Strategic Financial Management*, Prentice Hall, Hemel Hempstead.

COST MANAGEMENT

ost management is not merely about managing costs, but also value. It is about managing costs for both financial and competitive advantage, longer term as well as short term (Grundy 1998). To achieve these objectives a number of things need to be done simultaneously:

- manage costs for improved financial performance – balancing longer-term against shorter-term priorities,
- achieve this by adding to, rather than subtracting from, the business strategy,
- make explicit and continuing trade-offs between costs against value added – both externally and internally,
- prioritize expenditure against agreed, complementary, strategic and financial criteria, and
- identify, understand and manage key cost drivers, and relate these to the value drivers.

Some of the elements of this cost management philosophy are old and some are much newer. For instance, the problem of balancing longer-term against shorter-term priorities is a very old one. But explicitly linking to the business strategy and the competitive context in which value is created is newer still. Cost management should provide a disciplined and coherent framework for managing the cost process in a strategic rather than in a purely tactical manner.

This process is also inseparable from that of the process managing organizational change. It also involves managing the cost base in a way which is competitively targeted and benchmarked rather than just internal.

Cost management is applicable at the corporate, business, functional and project levels.

Its pros are:

- it can help to produce sufficient margins and profitability to grow the business, and
- it can generate innovation – in getting more out of the same, or less.

But one potential con is that too much focus on cost in isolation can severely harm the strategy, capability and morale (as at Marks & Spencer in the mid-1990s, which appears to have cut back on its services whilst competitors were increasing theirs, contributing to a later loss of market share).

Key techniques for cost management which we have already covered include:

- value and cost drivers, and
- AID analysis (for prioritizing costs).

In a later section ('Problem Diagnosis', p.249) we also cover fishbone analysis, which (as a special case) helps us to deal with diagnosis issues; for example, 'why are our IT costs too high?'

Gap analysis (see 'Business Planning', p.82) can also be useful, especially for:

- understanding what our unit costs are now (as compared to our competitors'), and
- where they need to be, say, in three years time (as compared with our future competitors' costs)

This could also bring in storytelling, competitor analysis and even an analysis of any future shifts in Porter's five competitive forces within the industry, which could increase the pressure on us to reduce our unit costs.

Also cost benchmarking against companies in other industries (for example for services costs) can be remarkably insightful, as it can help us become far more innovative in our thinking about cost.

Killer takeaways include:

- Practice again a zero-based thinking approach – what could your costs be if you were to re-assemble your resource base from scratch?
- Imagine the 'alien approach' – what would a new owner of the business, as if arriving from outer space, do with your cost base?

- Calculate some interesting analyses of specific unit costs to deliver a particular activity – for example a toilet seat on a space shuttle was once rumoured to cost over $3000, but why?

Cost management is linked to many other skills including:

- acquisition integration (p. 107) (which so often entails cost reduction),
- benchmarking (p. 111),
- business planning (p. 82),
- buying (p. 114) (to target supplier cost reductions),
- change management (p. 173),
- contract management (p. 86),
- controlling (p. 116),
- life-cycle management (p. 60),
- option generation (p. 249) (for cost-savings),
- resource management (p. 131),
- strategic thinking (p. 49),
- targeting goals (p. 100),
- turnaround (p. 158), and
- value management (p. 165).

Reference

Grundy, A.N. (1998) *Exploring Strategic Financial Management*, Prentice Hall, Hemel Hempstead (especially the chapter on 'Strategic Cost Management').

CREDIT CONTROL

C redit control is: 'The process of collecting debts on time – and with least hassle.'

To illustrate credit control, consider now both of the authors, who as part of their consulting business, actually need to be credit controllers. (One of the authors used to exercise that role too when he was finance director of a medium-sized retail wholesaler, many years ago. He had to collect the most difficult debts and picked up the tenacity to do it.)

Credit control is not a 'management-as-usual' activity, you have to be tough, resilient and tenacious. As a manager (unless you are in finance department) you may feel that it is not your job to pursue debts this way. But sales managers also have a big impact on credit control and should be skilled in credit control. Also, anyone setting up in their own business will almost certainly need to master these arts, especially as it is hard to chase both sales and money from debtors at the same time.

Probably left to their own devices only 60 per cent of the authors' invoices would get paid on time. As many as 10 per cent seem to get 'lost' and would be unpaid three or months later unless we were on to the case. (This is a great puzzle to us: is this an example of parallel universe opening up and gobbling up our invoices, never to be seen again? No, we think companies are sometimes less than competent.)

In 14 years trading we have not had a single bad debt, which is either fantastic luck, or perhaps because we are *awesome* in the art of credit control. It does help, of course, if your company has a distinctive competitive edge so that the threat of your non-supply does generate urgent payment, capitalizing on your bargaining power.

Whilst overly tight credit limits can be restrictive on the odd occasion, it is essential to be strict and highly focused on controlling credit and chasing money. We have already looked at the technique of analysing numbers of debtors (in sales terms) in 'Cash-flow Management' (p. 143), so it is appropriate here to focus more on a larger number of killer takeaways borne out of our own credit control experience:

- Chase for money *as soon as* it is overdue.
- Where a company has been late before, send a personal reminder in advance (say, mid-month) and ring them five days *before they are late*.
- Do not accept excuses about 'you just missed the payment run': if you were to threaten to put the company into receivership, they would quickly find a convenient cheque book.
- Small- and medium-sized enterprises can charge premium interest rates for invoices not paid after a certain number of days (you can remind them of this, if you are an SME).
- If your customer is a plc, get their accounts and identify statements about 'corporate values', and refer to these, to increase the sense that they are not fulfilling their corporate duty.
- Send regular statements, making them colourful (yellow and red rings around late invoices look pretty, and quite powerful).
- Become awesome through a carefully graduated process of escalation. Your first call can be very relaxed, the second a bit less so – and so on – until the fifth one has reached DEFCON THREE (that state of readiness before nuclear war begins).
- Use a geometric series to schedule your calls: plan your calls firstly spaced out two days apart, then a day, then half a day, then one and a half hours, then forty five minutes, then twenty, then ten, then five minutes, then continuously. Now you are totally focused on collecting the money, nothing else matters anymore … (we would hate to be on the receiving end of this treatment – which is reserved for companies with a precarious financial position).
- Vary who you telephone first – go to the financial controller, then the finance director, the managing director, head office, financial director, ever upwards.

So do you begin to get the idea?

Actually, whilst not so high in the pecking order of management skills, credit control is both demanding and requires a lot of thought – and learning.

Key links between credit control and other skills include:

- cash-flow management (p. 143),
- drive (p. 266),
- influencing (p. 211),
- negotiating (p. 92),
- proactivity (p. 281),
- problem diagnosis (p. 254),

- stakeholder management (p. 199) (within the company),
- stress management (p. 289) (in this case causing it), and
- understanding company accounts (p. 160).

FINANCIAL AWARENESS

A part from qualified accountants, many managers feel slightly nervous about finance, flocking over the years to learn about balance sheets and profit and loss accounts.

Unfortunately that is often where it ends – you have broken the 'balance sheet barrier,' but so what? This will only give a snapshot of the financial position, but tells you nothing about the future. There is a less thorough knowledge about using financial analysis-for-decision making, e.g. investment appraisal (see 'Project Appraisal', p. 98), which is a great pity. For most managers, understanding how to evaluate future decisions is more important than understanding external reports and accounts.

Financial awareness can be defined as: 'The understanding of your company's (and your department's) past and current financial results, and also of its future financial potential – and the factors impacting on this potential.'

Financial awareness is needed for all business plans, business cases and project appraisal. It is particularly important when making acquisitions or entering into alliances. The techniques of discounted cash flow are especially relevant, too, for evaluating divestment options.

When making export/import decisions, awareness of the impact of adverse currency movements is also crucial, as these can have a huge and unfortunate impact on business profitability.

Financial awareness is also an important skill for judging the profitability of competitors, and equally for understanding the financial health of customers and suppliers.

Financial awareness breaks down into:

- balance sheet understanding (often not the most important thing to know about – as we said earlier),
- profit and loss account,
- return on capital,
- cash flow,
- management accounts,

- investment appraisal (including discounted cash flow and net present values),
- financing instruments, and
- other treasury issues, like foreign exchange and esoteric financial instruments like futures and options.

In many ways it is more important – in order to achieve more advanced financial awareness – to be able to link financial results to the underlying drivers: the growth drivers, performance drivers, the five forces, value and cost drivers etc.

Killer takeaways:

- Break even is a bad benchmark – if used in isolation. At the break-even point you are actually destroying shareholder value, unless you have zero capital employed, or have a zero cost of capital (which are most unlikely possibilities).
- Where financial performance is weak, use 'fishbone analysis' (see 'Problem Diagnosis', p.254) to understand its root causes.

Financial awareness is central to:

- budgeting (p.141),
- business cases (p.79),
- business planning (p.82),
- cash-flow management (p.143),
- controlling (p.116),
- cost management (p.146),
- economic awareness (macro, p.30 and micro, p.33),
- financial planning (p.154),
- life-cycle management (p.60),
- margin management (p.88),
- negotiating (p.92),
- resource management (p.131),
- risk and uncertainty analysis (p.44), and
- turnaround (p.158).

References

Grundy, A.N. (1998) *Exploring Strategic Financial Management*, Prentice Hall, Hemel Hempstead.
Grundy, A.N. (2002) *Shareholder Value*, Capstone Press, Oxford.

FINANCIAL PLANNING

F inancial planning can be defined as: 'The process of integrating future revenue, cost investment and cash-flow plans to produce detailed future financial projections.'

Since the advent of spreadsheets, financial planning has been more able to take into account variability in possible results, which is a great help. Software packages are now so much more powerful and flexible. When they were first introduced one of the authors needed to leave his financial model computing for *nearly ten minutes* to accomplish a single sensitivity analysis. (He was able to go to the loo, have a cup of coffee, have a chat, and come back – and still find that it had not finished computing the numbers.)

Unfortunately, the very slickness of modern software, which makes the author's experience almost unrecognizable, has meant that financial planning can become an end in itself. Financial modelling in particular (once described as the corporate equivalent of a 'rain dance' – or a magical ritual) – thrives on scenarios and sensitivity analysis – but is often used as a kind of corporate valium to reduce managers' anxiety about the future and about future financial performance.

Sensitivity analysis – or seeing what the impact is of, say, a plus or minus five or ten per cent variance on a particular variable – is often then reduced to 'insensitivity' analysis; the latter involves deciding the answer you want to get, and then manipulating the variables to show that you can still get to the right answer.

The more obvious techniques for doing financial planning thus include profitability (cash-flow projections, spread sheets, discounted cash flows, and sensitivity analyses). But the less obvious techniques involve using other techniques, which we have already covered, including:

- growth drivers,
- five competitive forces, and
- the uncertainty grid (coupled with proper scenario storytelling) – see 'Risk and Uncertainty Analysis', p. 44).

Killer takeaways include:

- Beware naïve use of NPV or net presentation. Without using the more qualitative techniques mentioned above (like the uncertainty grid) it becomes effectively 'numbers prevent vision' – or numbers for their own sake.
- Always ask yourself in formulating or reviewing your assumption the question 'what is the one big thing we have forgotten?'.

Financial planning relates to a host of other key skills, including:

- budgeting (p. 141),
- business cases (p. 79),
- business planning (p. 82),
- forecasting (p. 156),
- life-cycle management (p. 60),
- market research (p. 66),
- project appraisal (p. 98),
- risk and uncertainty analysis (p. 44),
- storytelling (p. 47), and
- turnaround (p. 158).

FORECASTING

 orecasting is about trying to understand future demand (and the factors driving it), as a preliminary to more detailed financial planning. Forecasting was a very big management fashion in the 1960s and early 1970s, when long range planning was in vogue. Forecasting can be used:

- to understand macro economic or industry trends,
- to understand market trends,
- to protect product sales,
- to anticipate future demand, customer-by-customer, or distribution channel by distribution channel, and
- to predict labour skills needs.

The pros of forecasting are that:

- it can help you to look around corners, particularly if it is able to incorporate change and discontinuities, and
- it can prepare you for either more adverse market conditions, or for buoyant ones which suddenly take off, creating capability problems.

But a major con of forecasting can be that it becomes primarily a projection of past trends, which may be inappropriate guides to the future.
Key forecasting techniques include:

- the (more qualitative) strategy techniques, like PEST factors, growth drivers, the five competitive forces, motivator and hygiene factors,
- the uncertainty grid, and
- identifying turning points in the market (for example, the UK house market peaking during late 2002/early 2003) and transitional events such as a potential change in government, or a major market restructuring, or a regulatory change.

Key takeaways include:

- Avoid 'T-minus-one' thinking. Here, your thinking about the future is a reflection not so much of the future – or even the present – but of the past.
- Once again, what is the one big thing you have forgotten? (As when BMW did not anticipate the UK exchange rate strengthening by over 20 per cent after it had acquired Rover Group.)

Key linkages to other skills include:

- competitor awareness (p. 25),
- customer awareness (p. 57),
- economic awareness (macro, p. 30 and micro, p. 33),
- financial planning (p. 154),
- market awareness (p. 62),
- project appraisal (p. 98),
- storytelling (p. 47), and
- strategic thinking (p. 49).

TURNAROUND

T urnaround is a very specialist activity (like acquisitions management) requiring a very high order of skills. Turnarounds are situations where a business or a department has lost its way, and this is now reflected in poor financial performance (and, possibly, losses and cash-flow deficits). Whilst we have included this in the financial skills section it requires many other skills too (such as leadership, strategy, change management etc.). The basic principles of turnaround management are twofold:

1 you need to save the company short term, from failure, and
2 you also need to develop a view of its medium, and longer-term strategic potential.

Key techniques for turnaround are:

- Performance drivers analysis, and also fishbone analysis (see 'Problem Diagnosis', p. 254) – for more detailed analysis of why the company/department needs turning around.
- Competitive benchmarking – using motivator/hygiene factor analysis and competitor profiling.
- Financial analysis (including key ratios – and trends).
- Analysis of industry structure (and trend) analysis – with Porter's five forces and growth driver analysis, and of the company's own capability.
- The strategic option grid (see 'Option Generation', p. 249) – for exploring ways of turning it around.

The turnaround manager thus needs to have very strong drive, analytical skills, be a natural leader and change manager, besides also being astute financially and commercially skilled.

Killer takeaways include:

- Identify – if the company was ever a success – why this was the case?
- Think of your own role as turnaround manager as being that of a surgeon – you need to take necessary action in order to secure survival and future health of the patient.
- Remember that operations are painful – so act in as humane a way as is possible, and try to do as much as possible in one turnaround phase – especially restructuring.

Turnaround is closely linked with the following skills:

- business planning (p. 82),
- change management (p. 173),
- cost management (p. 146),
- direction setting (p. 179),
- divestment (p. 28),
- financial planning (p. 154),
- motivating (p. 192),
- negotiation (p. 92) (with financiers),
- organizational design (p. 218),
- performance analysis (p. 94),
- problem diagnosis (p. 254),
- resource management (p. 131),
- targeting goals (p. 100), and
- understanding company accounts (p. 160).

UNDERSTANDING COMPANY ACCOUNTS

 ompany accounts are complex and hard to get to grips with. But this is not necessarily impossible provided that a step-by-step process is applied.

Understanding company accounts is needed:

- to diagnose your own performance, or
- to diagnose the performance of competitors, customers or suppliers (for instance, to see if there is any real risk of insolvency).

Company accounts can be understood as a nine-stage process. (Grundy 1998)

Step 1 – Do an overall review of the five-year record

You should first start with the company's five-year review. The reason for beginning with the five-year review (which is usually buried at the back of the report) is that it is helpful to pick up a quick picture of trends before you look at the detailed financial performance. This high-level review will help to identify, for example:

- any uneven past trading record,
- the impact of any exceptional (or extraordinary) items, and
- the existence of any longer-term trends in margins or operating profit (and cost levels).

Step 2 – Do a quick review of current year's and last year's profits

It is now time to examine recent trading performance. This involves a quick glance at the current year's profit (and the comparative figure(s)). You do not always have to work out a large number of different financial ratios to discern the really key trends. For instance, if expenses are rising generally faster than the rate of growth in turnover then this should be spotted without actually computing financial ratios. Also, a quick glance will reveal any major exceptional (or one-off) items. The regular incidence of exceptional items might suggest performance in the future may be disappointing, too.

Step 3 – Do a quick review of directors' review and highlights

There is always a wealth of questions that can be raised by reading the chairman's and the chief executive's statements and the financial highlights, which occur in the first few pages of the report. The statements of top managers will often shed light on the current business strategies and tactics that are impacting on financial performance. You should first consider trends in operating profit and then analyse some key expense ratios. (A word of warning here: you will need to extract the relevant details from the more detailed notes to the annual report and accounts. This requires a degree of ferreting out. But always remember that there is no point in doing ratio analysis because a ratio can be calculated. Always ask: what are you seeking to learn from it?)

Step 4 – Probing the balance sheet for financial health

You will have to read the balance sheet in unison with the notes to the accounts – otherwise you will easily pick up the wrong numbers and may also miss important downsides, for example, buried in notes on 'contingent liabilities'.

You should work steadily through the balance sheet, for example to consider:

- The effective use of assets: stocks, fixed assets relative to turnover (you can also look at the number of people relative to turnover from a profit and loss account note). Also, you should examine the number of days of unpaid turnover effectively tied up in debtors.

Stretching out credit terms may be one symptom of underlying financial and competitive malaise.
- Liquidity – here you should compute liquidity ratios and gearing.
- The level of 'gearing' or the ratio of long-term debt to total risk capital.
- The number of debtors' days outstanding, and level of stock relative to activity levels.
- Creditor strain – how high are *trade* creditors relative to annual value of bought-in goods and services.
- The cash-flow statement, which highlights how cash positive or negative trading operations are, and also the extent to which this is sufficient to fund investment or whether the company is sucking-in vast amounts of new capital from outside.

Step 5 – Calculating the profit

Now calculate profit before interest and tax, and then divide it by capital employed to find your return on capital (or ROCE). For example:

	Example (£m)
Profit before interest and tax (or 'PBIT')	15 *
Interest	4
Profit after interest and before tax	11
Tax	3
Profit after interest and tax	8
Net assets	60 (equals shareholders' funds)
Longer-term liabilities	25

To calculate ROCE take * as our defined 'profit' as follows:

$$\text{ROCE} = \frac{\text{Profit before interest and tax (PBIT)}}{\text{Net assets} + \text{Longer term liabilities}}$$

$$\text{ROCE} = \frac{15}{(60 + 25)} = 17.6\%$$

Step 6 – The cash-flow statement

In examining the cash-flow statement:

- examine whether the net cash inflow from operating activities overall *is positive,* and
- review whether net cash inflows from operating activities exceeds (or is on a par with) the annual cost investing activities (unless the company is easily able to raise money from external sources of finance).

Step 7 – How are the financial position and prospects interrelated – what are the key business drivers?

What overall pattern is now revealed about current financial health and business performance? Is the company drifting strategically or, alternatively, has it moved aggressively into ill-thought-through ventures? Is its financial success based on (temporarily) favourable market and competitive conditions that might now be crumbling.

Step 8 – What future strategic and financial prospects exist?

Further key questions which help to identify the future prospects of a company are:

- Considering its past profit growth – is this growth of profits sustainable?
- What do future strategies for business development reveal? (Consider statements made by the Board on the future, details of the company's capital programmes, and so on).
- What management strengths exist?

Step 9 – Summarize and conclude

In our final step you should summarize the half-a-dozen key insights gleaned from your analysis. This should yield an overall prognosis, and future prospects, and be set against the strategic context.

Killer takeaways are:

- Read accounts backwards – look at the five-year track record *first*, to gain an overview of past trends.
- Relate the level of profitability/other trends to your industry knowledge and to your wider knowledge of the company. Do the figures make sense intuitively?

Understanding company accounts is closely related to:

- all of the 'strategy' and 'marketing' skills (p. 13ff and p. 53ff),
- controlling (p. 116),
- financial awareness (p. 152), and
- performance analysis (p. 94).

Reference

Grundy, A.N. (1998) *Exploring Strategic Financial Management*, Prentice Hall, Hemel Hempstead – especially the chapter on 'Strategic Financial Accounting'.

VALUE MANAGEMENT

I n *Shareholder Value*, value management is defined as being: 'The present value of the future cash flows of a company, or of a particular project or decision.' (Grundy 2002)

In essence, this definition focuses on shareholder value primarily from a management perspective, as management (at least in theory) *ought* to have a clearer view of the economic prospects of the business than someone on the outside of the company.

Naturally, outsiders too have some view of the company's prospects, and it is their expectations of future performance – combined with signals given by management and from generally known market trends – which determine most movements in share price.

Because of the volatility of share prices, proponents of shareholder value management tend to emphasize the importance of getting the internal view of value creation right rather than spending the majority of the time massaging the external share price. In their view, positive share price movements will follow on naturally from excellent performance by the company in generating superior future cash flows. (Investor PR exercises, smoothing the annual profits, or earnings per share and dividend growth are here seen to be of more secondary importance.)

Value management is thus the process of managing shareholder value – both for short- and longer-term gains.

Shareholder value is therefore highly relevant to:

- corporate strategy,
- business strategy,
- acquisitions/alliances and investment,
- project appraisal, and
- change management.

Its pros are:

- it gives a very real focus in an organization – on economic benefits rather than on 'we fancy doing this', and
- it can help to avoid shareholder value being destroyed – at every level.

Its cons are:

- It is often badly misunderstood, and is sometimes used primarily as a means of applying pressure to achieve shorter-term performance targets.
- It can become another layer of bureaucracy, or a fad.

The key techniques of shareholder value management include value and cost drivers, and also EVA discounted or economic value added and discounted cash flow (to which we now turn). (Stern Stewart) Economic Value Added (EVA) can be defined more specifically as shown in the following equation:

EVA = (rate of return – cost of capital) × capital employed

For example, if a company's net operating profit after tax is £250,000 and its capital is £1,000,000 (and thus its rate of return is 25%), and its cost of capital is 15%, then:

EVA = (25% – 15%) × £1,000,000
= 10% x £1,000,000
= £100,000

EVA is thus residual income (after deducting the cost of capital).

In order to improve EVA, then, one could either generate more operating income, reduce the tax charge, or reduce the cost of capital. The key point of EVA is that it actually provides a better focus for measuring and managing corporate and business performance than conventional accounting measures.

Net present value takes the future stream of cash flows of a business as if it were a project and adjusts for the fact that these cash flows will occur in the future, and will thus have less value than present ones. This lower value can be due to a number of factors, including:

- inflation, plus
- business risk and uncertainty, plus
- the 'time value of money'.

(See the example in 'Project Appraisal' p. 98 for more details.)

In managing for value exercises, not merely are projects appraised using discounted cash flow, but entire businesses too.

Killer takeaways include the following:

- Be prepared to ask the question 'what is the value of "shareholder value management"' – otherwise it can become a value-destroying ritual.
- Don't do anything in management unless you have asked the key question, 'what shareholder (or economic) value can I foresee coming out of this?'

Value management is related to:

- all the strategy skills (p. 13ff) (especially acquisitions and divestment),
- business planning (p. 82),
- cash-flow management (p. 143),
- financial planning (p. 154),
- project appraisal (p. 98),
- turnaround (p. 158), and
- understanding company accounts (p. 160).

Reference

Bennett, Stewart G. III. (1991) *The Quest for Value – The EVA Management Guide*, HarperBusiness, NY.

Grundy, A.N., (2002) *Shareholder Value*, Capstone Press, Oxford. (Part of the *Express Exec* series.)

Leadership Skills 7

CHAIRING

C hairing a meeting is a very important skill, especially if you wish to become more senior in the organization. Chairing involves: 'Being responsible for co-ordinating the discussions of a group of management in order to reach a pre-targeted goal, and to add value generally.'

Chairing is not a bureaucratic activity but it involves interpersonal skills of a high order. It entails:

- Ensuring that there is some form of agenda.
- Encouraging balanced input from all members of the team so that no single person dominates, and that everyone contributes.
- Keeping track of time, so that if the agenda cannot realistically be adequately covered, this is flagged up.
- Stepping into the debate – in the event that there is disruption.
- Trying to draw out any hidden causes of disagreement between individuals to the surface.

A formal chairperson is essential at a meeting where the decisions being taken are going to be relatively complex. It is also imperative where a group meets regularly, or where the focus for discussion is on a particular, ongoing project.

The pros of chairing a meeting are:

- it gives it more structure and flow, and
- it (usually) will make it less disruptive.

A possible con is that it can (inadvertently, and with the wrong style of chairperson) make it bureaucratic.

Chairing requires a number of basic techniques:

- having a pre-set agenda, or setting one out at the outset (key questions are often a better way of accomplishing this than more bureaucratic bullet points),
- establishing some ground rules, for example that 'politics are not allowed' at this session (see 'Facilitation', p. 82),
- allocating time (at least approximately) to topics, and
- deciding in advance what will be done (by whom and by when) – if not all agenda items are thoroughly covered.

Killer takeaways on chairing meetings include:

- remove all chairs – this can accelerate proceedings hugely,
- those arriving more than three minutes late get a yellow card, those arriving more than six minutes late get a red card, and
- bring a little model helicopter to wave at attendees if there are patches of conversation which are irrelevant, or over-detailed or unnecessarily anecdotal (the helicopter signifies the need to maintain the mode of helicopter thinking). Or use some other prop or play to energize and focus conversation, to avoid it becoming yet another management ritual.

Other skills that chairing relates to include:

- energizing (p. 184),
- helicopter thinking (p. 40),
- prioritization (p. 277),
- stakeholder management (p. 199), and
- summarizing (p. 202).

CHANGE MANAGEMENT

hange management is now defined as: 'The systematic pursuit of new and different states of organizational structure skills, mindset behaviours and mindsets.'

Change management is appropriate when:

- the environment is changing, both significantly and (potentially) disruptively,
- where you wish to proactively pre-position yourself in advance of pending, or inevitable organizational change, and
- for acquisition integration.

Change management is a good idea when:

- there is a clear strategy for the change,
- there is a robust business case for the change, and
- where the change is a positive good for the organization generally (or what Tesco call 'positive change').

Change management is not so good an idea when:

- it has unclear objectives, and
- it is aimed at implementing some new management trend which has not been thought through – like business process re-engineering (BPR), or the balanced score card – which may not be well suited to the organization, or where it is unclear how its assumed benefits will be captured.

A technique for change management is 'from–to' analysis (see Fig. 8.1, p. 209). This separates out the old situation from the new and desired situation. The old situation and new situation are scored between 1 and 5 – these scores symbolize a particular state of the organization.

From–to (FT) analysis is useful for both targeting and monitoring strategic change. Another key technique for change management is 'forcefield' analysis, which we turn to next.

Forcefield analysis is a technique which brings to the surface the underlying forces which may accelerate a particular change, or retard it, or even move the change backwards. These forces can be separately identified as 'enablers' or 'constraints'. But neither set of positive or negative forces can be adequately identified without first specifying the objectives of the implementation.

Forcefield analysis represents the relative strength of each individual enabling or constraining force by drawing an arrowed line whose length is in proportion to that of its relative strength.

A horizontal version of forcefield analysis is depicted in Fig. 7.1. Note in this case that, on balance, the enabling forces appear less strong than the constraining forces. This particular analysis is for a telecommunication company's strategic plan. It shows that although many of the plans, processes and programmes had been put in place, it was nevertheless difficult to envisage implementation being a complete success. Subsequent events suggested that implementation difficulties at the company were very severe.

As a rule of thumb, one would wish to see the enablers outweighing the constraints by a factor of at least 1.5 to 2 overall, in accordance with the principle of military dominance. Otherwise we should be concerned that implementation droop will set in.

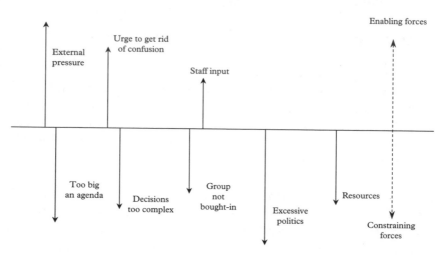

Fig. 7.1   Forcefield analysis – telecommunications company

Also, any stoppers really must be addressed, otherwise implementation really won't happen. During (and before) implementation the key implementation forces should be continually monitored to ensure that none threatens to go critical and become a stopper.

The key benefits of forcefield analysis are that it:

- encourages you to think about difficulty as opposed merely to attractiveness,
- helps you to focus on the context and process for implementation, rather than its context, and
- gives an early warning of 'mission impossible' projects.

The biggest downside of forcefield analysis is that it is sometimes too much of a snapshot of the short and medium term. This can be remedied however by a secondary technique called the 'difficulty-over-time curve' (see Fig. 7.2), which helps you draw a line projecting the complexity over the change. Killer takeaways on change management include:

- Always ask yourself the question: 'what is the economic value of pursuing a particular area of change?'
- Are any of the constraints likely to become a stopper?
- Use the difficulty-over-time curve to understand how the dynamics of implementation might change.

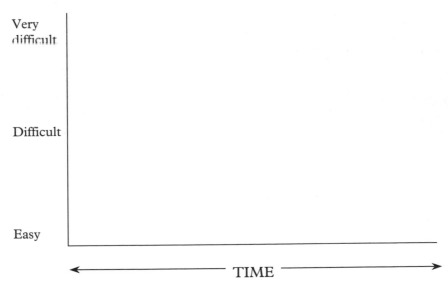

Fig. 7.2 Difficulty-over-time curve

Change management is linked to many other skills, including:

- all of the strategy skills (p. 13ff),
- acquisition integration (p. 107),
- cost management (p. 146),
- motivating (p. 192),
- organizational design (p. 218),
- organization and people planning (p. 220),
- option generation (p. 249),
- problem diagnosis (p. 254),
- resource management (p. 131),
- stakeholder management (p. 199), and
- turnaround (p. 158).

COACHING

Coaching can be defined as: 'The process of helping an individual develop on a one-to-one basis – with a mentor or coach.'

Coaching is appropriate for new staff joining an organization, for high potential (but usually younger managers), and also for middle and senior level managers who are facing new challenges outside their traditional competency set.

The pros of coaching are that it:

- gives an individual a lot more confidence in dealing with issues,
- provides more specific help to develop their skills in critical areas, and
- can be accomplished privately, so that the manager doesn't have to feel, or be seen as being, inadequate or lacking in competence.

The potential cons of coaching are that:

- it is often difficult to find a coach with the competence and style which will fit the managers specific needs, and
- internal coaches who are senior often do not necessarily have the time or the inclination to carry out the duties of a coach effectively.

The authors have much experience of acting as coaches, and this can be a very rewarding job. Typically, one can cover anything between three to five times as much ground as, say, a conventional management development course. The flexibility and focus of coaching means that you can rapidly put a number of fires out – and it is a very short second of time. One manager who went through this process reflected, off her own back, on the value she had experienced through greater personal effectiveness:

'This is magic. Before I was working Saturdays and now not only have I cleared my weekend so I can see my kids but I have actually cleared Fridays for helicopter thinking, too.'

Killer takeaways on coaching include:

- see your coach *at least* once a month (and possibly even twice, if you are facing some really stiff challenge),
- focus the session on no more than three key issues at a time (unless it is longer than an hour), and
- maintain a helpline in the interim.

Coaching links to other key skills including:

- learning (p. 271),
- option generation (p. 249),
- political awareness (p. 196),
- prioritization (p. 277),
- problem diagnosis (p. 254),
- self-awareness (p. 285),
- self-development (p. 286),
- stress management (p. 289), and
- time management (p. 291).

Reference

Grundy, A.N. (2003a) *Developing the Individual*, Capstone Publishing, Oxford.

DIRECTION SETTING

D irection setting involves creating a vision and having an awareness of the alignment factors which are required to deliver this. These alignment factors can be ones either outside your scope of influence, or ones which you have partial influence over.

Direction setting is advantageous in order to energize managers, besides helping them to allocate and prioritize resources (and projects), and to deliver shareholder value. But where the direction is an inappropriate one, or is ill-thought through this can actually be disadvantageous.

A key technique for direction setting is wishbone analysis, which we already saw in 'Product Development' section (p 69). This enables us to:

- identify the vision (at the very left of the wishbone),
- list the alignment factors (the bones of the wishbone),
- diagnose how important/uncertain these are (perhaps with the uncertainty grid),
- gain more influence over these where your influence is relatively low, and
- monitor their ongoing alignment.

Direction doesn't always need to be set in a definitive mode, or a 'deliberate strategy' (Mintzberg 1994) or where the objective and the plan are well defined and detailed. You may also find the direction emerging more gradually according to new opportunities arising in the environment, or creating an 'emergent strategy' (Mintzberg 1994).

The pros of a deliberate strategy are that it:

- gives a clear sense of direction,
- can give you a very real competitive advantage,
- can optimize the use of your resources, and reduce politics, and
- can be energizing.

The cons of this can be that it:

- may be inflexible, and
- may be an inappropriate strategy to pursue, anyway.

The pros of an emergent strategy are that it:

- gives you greater flexibility, and
- is often better at coping with an uncertain environment.

The cons of emergent strategy are, however, that it:

- can waste resources, and
- can be very confusing and de-energizing.

A further form of strategy is that of 'contingent strategy'. This is particularly useful for direction setting where there are uncertain conditions. A contingent strategy is one which will be committed to if, and only if, certain conditions in the world line up. In other ways, it will not actually crystallize as a decision until the context is appropriate.

Some strategies like acquisitions are already of that nature; you would not for instance, decide to do it until the price was right, the due diligence was OK, etc. But there may be many other projects of that nature which are either currently within a deliberate strategy, but perhaps should not be, or are emergent, but should be thought through a lot deeper.

Killer takeaways now include:

- be clear, be simple, be direct – do not beat about the bush, and
- tell people not just what your strategy is, but what it is not going to be, too.

Direction setting as a skill links to many others, including:

- all the strategy skills (p. 13ff),
- all the marketing skills (p. 53ff),
- business planning (p. 82),
- drive (p. 266),
- energizing (p. 184),
- option generation (p. 249),
- policy setting (p. 194),

- proactivity (p. 281),
- stakeholder management (p. 199), and
- turnaround (p. 158).

Reference

Mintzberg, H., (1994) *The Rise and Fall of Strategic Planning*, Prentice Hall, Hemel Hempstead.

EMPATHIZING

mpathizing is an important skill involving seeing things from the perspective of others. Empathizing entails understanding their cognitive and emotional agendas.

The pros of empathizing are that:

- it enables you to gain rapport more easily with key stakeholders, and thus to influence them,
- it also opens you up *to be influenced* by them, thus giving you more behavioural flexibility, and
- it means that you are more likely to reach agreement easily – where there are areas of disagreement.

When negotiating, however, it may be unwise to empathize too much with the other parties – for example on an acquisition, on alliance, or in contract negotiation.

A key technique of empathizing is to use the levels of agendas (see Fig. 7.3). This reminds us to explore not merely the surface agendas but also the deeper ones too, right down to someone's unconscious anxieties and drivers. Is who you are talking to, anxious about their job, or concerned about being sidelined by a colleague.

Empathizing is applicable to:

- any sales situation,
- dealing with any difficult person (why are they being so difficult?), and
- facilitating any communications.

Fig. 7.3 Levels of agendas

Key skills which empathizing links to include:

- coaching (p. 177),
- interviewing (p. 213),
- listening (p. 190),
- motivating (p. 192),
- performance appraisal (p. 222),
- political awareness (p. 196), and
- stakeholder management (p. 199).

ENERGIZING

nergizing is another one of the softer skills which is a counter-balance to the large number of our more tangible manageable skills. Energizing can be defined as: 'Raising the energy levels of an individual, a team, a department or an entire organization.' Energizing is appropriate:

- after any major organizational change,
- during any more difficult project,
- when leading a team, and
- when mobilizing a strategy.

Energizing is advantageous when:

- there have been major distractions or disruptions to implementation,
- the organization is growing very quickly, or is simply running flat out, and
- resources have had to be reduced, or deployed in the organization.

Energizing may involve some special techniques, some of them which might seem somewhat off the wall, but can be rather effective, including:

- During an away-day, having a five-minute (and possibly unscheduled) break. This not only provides some time out, but actually gets more energy to the brain.
- Do some yoga. At Cranfield School of Management, one of the tutors got managers to do some early morning yoga – which is fantastic not just at reducing stress, but in moving energy around the body. 'Salute to the sun' is a favourite warm-up sequence – you feel red hot and raring to go after doing this sequence a mere three or four times.
- One of the authors once had to run a series of one-and-a-quarter hour classes (four in a day) with 50 MBA students each time. The session was exactly the same format, making it repetitive, hard to be spontaneous with, and particularly difficult because you could not easily

remember what you said this time versus last time. Like indulging in sexual activity, the first time might be fantastic, the second time great, the third time a lot harder, and the fourth time ... The solution he found, in order to re-energize, was to have a half-hour Shiatsu massage after the second or third session. (Shiatsu gives an astonishing surge of energy through the body about 20 to 30 minutes afterwards.)
• In summary, find what works for you.

Killer takeaways for energizing are:

• plot your energy-over-time curve (Fig. 7.4) so you are aware of energy dips and take steps to avoid draining your deeper energy reservoirs,
• avoid indulging in very heavy food at lunchtime, and alcohol,
• take some exercise and get some fresh air – at the middle of each day,
• go to the gym – regularly, and
• learn how to wind down – stress dissipates energy enormously.

Energizing links to a number of key skills including:

• acquisition integration (p. 107),
• coaching (p. 177),
• direction setting (p. 179),
• drive (p. 266),
• facilitation (p. 186), and
• motivating (p. 192).

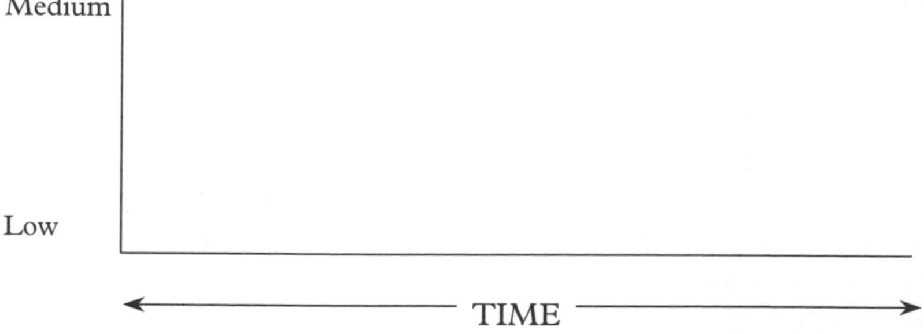

Fig. 7.4 Energy-over-time curve

FACILITATION

acilitation can be defined as: 'The process of accelerating a decision-making process, or of diminishing its difficulty, or of improving the quality of the final results.'

Facilitation has a number of pros:

- it can deliver spectacularly – through achieving more effective results,
- it can help a team come up with life-saving conclusions which they would not have arrived at otherwise, and
- it can help avoid stressful and irreversibly painful experiences.

Facilitation also has a number of cons:

- it can be extremely hard to find a really good facilitator,
- it can be costly to employ someone outside the organization, and
- it can be risky to use an internal facilitator, who may lack sufficient perceived independence and credibility to do the job.

Amplifying the first point above, one of the authors gained second-hand experience from an external facilitator. His task was to be the catalyst for developing a company's strategy in the healthcare sector. It was said (by observers) that he ran out of steam, failed to inject the necessary energy, resorting to periodic blasts of:

'*Watch out, watch out* – the elephants are coming!'

– presumably referring to the company's competitors.

To illustrate the third bullet point (the difficulty of finding a good, internal facilitator), one (internal) facilitator was observed by the authors – whilst he was conducting management research. As facilitator, flip-chart pen in hand, he appeared to misrepresent what one of the other managers had said. This manager took personal offence to this, and her acidic and instantaneous (and, indeed, personal) attack on the facilitator was the equivalent of a Sky TV horror movie, where an innocent-looking, beautiful young lady turns into an alien vampire, flies across the room, and promptly rips open the throat of her enemy, causing instant death.

The result of the internal facilitator's misrepresentation was to halt the session in its tracks. Perhaps the internal facilitator genuinely mistook what he/she said, or maybe decided to put a slight spin on it. In any event, the results were somewhat unpleasant. To be fair, this internal facilitator was playing too many (possibly conflicting) roles: being first of all a member of the management team and also being asked to act in a neutral way, effectively disenfranchising them. The temptation to cast just a little bit of a vote cost him dearly.

The solution (if you are ever a facilitator), is to signal quite clearly that:

> 'What I am about to say is not as a facilitator, but is my personal input to the debate, and now having said this, I now step quickly back into my facilitator's role.'

The above suggests that facilitation is indeed, a high-order skill. As authors, we would like now to make some twin contributions:

Tony:
'I was once interviewed by a researcher of Neuro-Linguistic Programming or NLP who wanted to understand my taken-for-granted competencies as a facilitator. These were no less than about 20 sub-skills, one of them being to inject humour to lighten an otherwise difficult and threatening situation (for example, by using a yellow card as a warning for non-functional behaviour).'

Laura:
'As a facilitator, my most difficult challenge was to facilitate the redesign of the trolley which is used to deliver groceries from supplier's storage facilities to grocery supermarkets. At the session I had the representatives from the major supermarkets, some major suppliers, and also the haulage companies (up to 50 stakeholders in all). The room was full of disparate groups of people with divergent agendas. There had been no real time to set up formal process with some key questions, nor with some process techniques, or anything, and even car parking to get to the meeting was problematic.'

'So I drew from my experience of chairing meetings from the pharmaceutical industry. I then got strong, I took charge, I ordered the haulage people to stop moving around in the room (their understandably natural habit) and managed to give the group some focus.'

As a facilitator, you will see from the above that you sometimes need to take a lot of power, but that you need to wield it, as best as you can, neutrally.

One method of doing this (attributable to Dave King, then of Dowty Case Communications a former client) is the 'P' behaviours:

- Brainstorm (at the beginning of a session) the 'P' behaviours that you do not want to have, like:
  - political,
  - personal,
  - picking,
  - pedantic, and
  - procrastinating.
- Get people to buy into not having these behaviours.
- When these behaviours begin to surface challenge any individuals exhibiting them, so that they do not take over the session which you are facilitating.

Killer takeaways from facilitating are:

- Tell scenario stories about how this particular session will go well or won't go well or sometimes will – into the future.
- Identify those individuals who are potentially neutral or difficult (either from their body language, or from their energies if ever you can sense them – see Grundy and Brown 2003) and also where they are coming from.
- Take power as appropriate.

Facilitation skills link to many other skills, including:

- all of the strategy and monitoring skills,
- acquisition integration,
- change management,
- project management,
- team building, and
- turnaround.

Reference

Grundy, A.N. & Brown, L. (2003), *Value-Based HR Strategy*, Butterworth Heinnemann.

LISTENING

L istening is a crucial skill for any manager or leader. Listening entails: 'Giving another person enough time and space to communicate what they are thinking and feeling.'

During listening you are mainly quiet, with the exception of making encouraging comments or inviting further exploration of ideas and feelings by asking questions. The important thing with listening is that you stay primarily with the other person's perspective rather than your own. Listening also involves body language that is open and encouraging – suggesting genuine interest. Here, appropriate eye contact is important: not too little, so that the person doesn't feel that you are not genuinely interested, and also not too much, so that your gaze is not too intense.

Listening is thus a very active activity, demanding considerable attention and thought – it is certainly not an activity where you switch off. In a situation where a group of people are the listeners, like a team of consultants, it is crucial to have some clear roles – otherwise the client will be concerned that you are not really adding value. For sure, this can really annoy the client, especially if they think the consultants' taxi meters are running.

Another useful way of showing that you are listening is to take some notes. This suggests (to the speaker) that what he/she is saying is of interest and of importance. This is even more powerful if you can periodically summarize what has come out of the speaker so far. Where the listener is a potential adviser to the speaker it will also be useful – after the speaker has got much of what they want to say off their chest – to start to feed in some ideas of your own. This can be done either as questions which suggest lines of enquiry, or by providing more specific ideas.

Killer takeaways include:

- Be continuously aware of the balance of conversation – if you are fact-finding, are you going dangerously over 40 per cent of your own input?
- Observe your listener's eye movements – dynamic movements suggest interest whilst blank stares suggest you have probably switched them off.

Listening links to a whole array of other business skills including:

- change management (p. 173),
- coaching (p. 177),
- customer awareness (p. 57),
- influencing (p. 211),
- questioning (p. 258),
- selling (p. 72), and
- stakeholder management (p. 199).

MOTIVATING

Motivating requires giving another person not just the energy to do something (see the previous section 'Energizing') but also providing them with a clear rationale to do something. It thus involves intervention at the emotional and mental levels, and also perhaps even at a political level. Motivating is always important, but particularly when there has been:

- a significant shock or disappointment within the organization, or
- a big high, or a major achievement in the organization, and from which point it is almost inevitable that there is likely to be a motivation dip.

To examine the importance of motivating one needs to look no further than that of the behaviour of football teams. At the time of writing, one of the authors' supported Arsenal (and continues to do so). Arsenal suffered major disappointments, losing to Blackburn (who were subsequently beaten 5–1 by Newcastle). They then drew against Chelsea in the quarter final of the FA cup. They then failed to qualify for the Champions League in Europe (quarter final), and to cap it all, their premiership lead over Manchester United slumped from eight points to minus three points at one stage.

Their manager, Arsène Wenger, together with their captain, Patrick Viera, breathed fresh life into the team and, even with injuries, managed to resume their lead and, with just ten men, beat Chelsea to resume their position. This motivation of the team would build on itself, helping avoid a cycle of decline in belief that they could continue to win.

Motivating is thus an intangible but vital ingredient in improving performance. It also demands more than shouting or throwing things at players (or at managers, even) – requiring an appeal to the deeper energies laying latent within them.

Whilst there are no fixed remedies for motivating managers, a number of tools can help you to understand the current situation, as a first step to instilling a fire and a desire in them to succeed.

One of these techniques is that of fishbone analysis (which we will see in the section 'Problem Diagnosis', p. 254). Here we define the symptom – at the right-hand side of the fishbone picture – working backwards to the left-hand side to its root causes.

Another technique is to analyse that particular stakeholder's agendas: these things which are turn-ons or turn-offs (or stakeholder agenda analysis – see Fig. 7.5). This should highlight the areas where you can most easily motivate, either by adding a new incentive for action, or removing an unnecessary turn-off.

Killer takeaways for motivating include:

- Using the stakeholder agenda analysis – what is the possible bait to make something irresistible in order to motivate positively?
- Using the stakeholder agenda analysis – what is the one big turn-off which, if removed, might make it possible to motivate someone?

These techniques can also be used for self-motivating oneself, as often one needs to reflect on one's own patterns of motivation.

Motivation links to a number of key business skills, including:

- change management (p. 173),
- coaching (p. 177),
- drive (p. 266),
- energizing (p. 184), and
- self-awareness (p. 285).

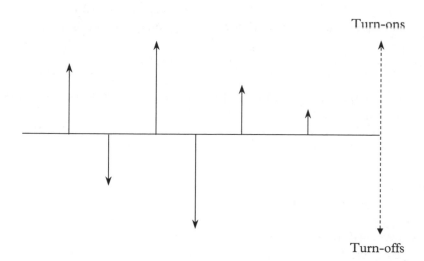

Fig.7.5 Stakeholder agenda analysis

POLICY SETTING

olicy setting entails the definition of general principles which the organization should follow. These might range from HR policies like equal opportunities and disciplinary process through to policies with regard to business class travel or how suppliers will be dealt with by the company.

Policy setting is complicated by the fact that you cannot always predict what circumstances are likely to come up. This means that besides drawing on past experience you also need to exercise a degree of imagination about the future. This may require some storytelling about the future environment, including some of the dilemmas which you are likely to face and particular situations which could occur.

Policy setting has a number of key advantages:

- it gives a framework for action, and for dealing with ambiguity – and in advance,
- it helps create a sense of fairness, and
- it makes it easier for the organization to solve difficulties – without having to escalate the decision up the management hierarchy.

But it can also have some considerable disadvantages:

- once set, a policy can be hard to change, and that policy might be inappropriate as the environment changes, and
- the policy might be exercised in a rigid way, causing both difficulty and value destruction.

Amplifying the first part above, Marks & Spencer had two major policies, which for years it would not give up; namely, that of having no changing rooms, and also not accepting other companies credit cards. This meant that it turned away a lot of sales, and annoyed a lot of customers over the years. On the other hand, the first policy store saved space (otherwise used for changing rooms) and the second policy also avoided credit card charges, which can run at over two per cent of turnover, and thus lost margins. But in the 1990s the costs of these policies overtook the benefits and M&S eventually – some would say belatedly – revised both of these policies.

There are no specific techniques as such for policy setting (other than those which we have covered in the strategy skills) so we shall now move directly on the same killer takeaways as follows:

- Decide not only the criteria for what you will do in the future, but also for what you won't do (for example, acquisition criteria).
- Decide how you will deal with things that you *might do,* remembering again the framework of 'contingent strategy' (see 'Direction Setting', p. 179).
- When formulating policies, try to illustrate them with specific examples rather than make them impenetrable and overly procedural.

Policy setting relates to other key business skills including:

- strategy skills (p. 13ff),
- direction setting (p. 179),
- imagination (p. 247),
- performance appraisal (p. 222),
- report writing (p. 227),
- recruiting (p. 225), and
- storytelling (p. 47).

POLITICAL AWARENESS

P olitical awareness can be defined as: 'The process of being aware of the political map around you, and of your own influence over your political environment.'

Political awareness has a number of key benefits, including:

- it enables you to get things done,
- it also helps you to avoid pursuing ideas and agendas that are 'no-hopers' in the organization,
- it will help you to move up the career ladder, either in your present or a future organization,
- it will help you to avoid the walls closing in on you, for instance during organizational downsizing, and losing your job, and
- if your company has been acquired it is absolutely an imperative: it is a fatal decision to be not only obstructive, but even neutral, vis-à-vis the new owners during this kind of situation.

Political awareness thus has many functions, and equally many pros, but there are also a number of possible cons, including:

- you can become oversensitive to political issues – the point where you do not pursue the fundamental goals (or needs) of the business, and
- you can gain a reputation for being over-political, and this can mean that people will co-operate with you less and less.

Political awareness is an intuitive skill, but is certainly one which can be enhanced by some analytical techniques. For instance, we have already covered the 'levels of agendas' of stakeholders, (Fig. 7.3, p. 183), and also stakeholder analysis (Fig. 7.5, p. 193). An additional technique, called 'stakeholder analysis (Fig. 7.7, p. 200), which we will explore in 'Stakeholder Management', brings these processes together.

In the present context, it is worthwhile nevertheless to introduce a further technique, known as 'influence–influence analysis'.

Also, it is possible to prioritize which stakeholders to focus on by plotting:

- *their* level of influenced on this issue, and
- *our* level of influence over them.

In Fig. 7.6 we see the two axes plotted. Note that one should try to evolve strategies for gaining more influence over those stakeholders who are most influential – and also those who we have currently least influence over.

Killer takeaways on political awareness are:

- Find the cunning plan for influencing people – what would make it irresistible to get them to do something, to think something, or to believe something?
- If you haven't got sufficient personal power to do something, either find a bigger source of power for yourself, or find some stakeholder within the organization who can do this for you.

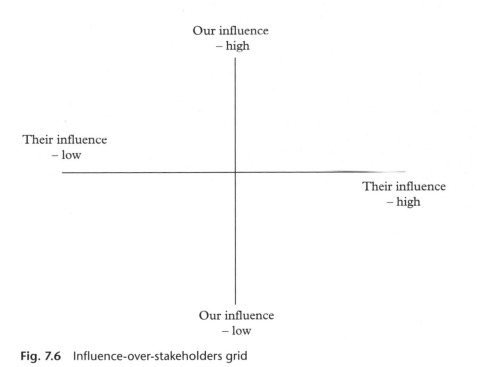

Fig. 7.6 Influence-over-stakeholders grid

Political awareness is linked to a number of both softer and harder skills, as we see below:

- acquisition integration (p. 107),
- change management (p. 173),
- helicopter thinking (p. 40),
- negotiating (p. 92),
- policy setting (p. 194),
- problem diagnosis (p. 254),
- risk and uncertainty analysis (p. 44),
- stakeholder management (p. 199),
- storytelling (p. 47), and
- strategic thinking (p. 49).

STAKEHOLDER MANAGEMENT

S takeholder management can be defined as: 'Managing the key stakeholders on a particular issue in order to take into account their agendas, and also to influence them in order to achieve your business (and possibly, personal) goals.'

Stakeholders are now defined as being: 'Those individuals or groups of individuals who are either the decision-makers, their advisers, the implementers, or the victims of what you (or others) are proposing to do.' Stakeholder management is essential in:

- helping to actively make critical decisions (rather than simply doing nothing),
- defusing and, if possible, dissolving organizational politics, and
- making policies actively discussible.

A classic way of managing stakeholders is to use the stakeholder analysis grid (Piercy 1991, Grundy & Brown 2002), which we accomplish as follows:

- *First*, identify who you believe the key stakeholders are at any phase of implementation.
- *Second*, evaluate whether these stakeholders have high, medium or low influence on the issue in question (you need to abstract this from their influence generally in the organization).
- *Third*, evaluate whether at the current time they are for the currently proposed action, against it, or idling in neutral (see Fig. 7.7).
- *Fourth*, examine the overall stakeholder picture to see what the 'so what?' is from it.
- *Fifth*, what is your cunning plan for repositioning various stakeholders?

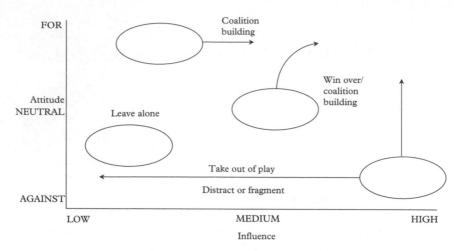

Fig. 7.7 Stakeholder analysis

Stakeholder analysis is useful:

- at the very start of a strategic process – even as early as the ideas stage,
- at the strategic options stage,
- when performing detailed planning,
- during mobilization of implementation,
- mid-way during, or at the latter stages of, implementation, and
- after implementation – to draw out the learning lessons.

Stakeholder analysis is also particularly useful for focusing on communication strategy. Here it will help you to identify which stakeholders to communicate with, when, how, and with what message.

The key benefits of stakeholder analysis are that:

- it deals effectively with political issues,
- it encourages mental agility and the ability to take a variety of perspectives on an issue, and
- it defuses organizational politics and makes particularly sensitive issues discussible, sometimes called (by some colleagues at Cranfield) 'the zone of uncomfortable debate' – or the ZUDE.

In order to estimate where a stakeholder is positioned approximately, you will need to see the world from that particular stakeholder's perspective. From experience over the years we have found that the best way to convey this is to ask managers to have in effect an out-of-body experience – not quite literally, of course!

Stakeholder management is linked with:

- acquisitions and alliances (p. 15ff),
- change management (p. 173),
- cost management (p. 146),
- direction setting (p. 179),
- influencing (p. 211),
- option generation (p. 249),
- political awareness (p. 196),
- recruitming (p. 225), and
- storytelling (p. 47).

SUMMARIZING

S ummarizing is a competence which, if mastered, is a distinctive management skill that can give you a significant career edge. Summarizing can be defined as: 'The ability to extract the essence from complex information and to present it in such a way that is easy to digest – but without oversimplifying it.'

Summarizing is thus a key communication skill. Besides being an essential part of making effective presentations its pros are that:

- you can focus discussion on these elements of your summary which appear to be most important, and/or interesting,
- you will focus the subsequent discussion of a group, and make it easier for them to generate more productive output from it, and also to make specific decisions, and
- you should come across as much more effective as a strategic thinker.

Summarizing is also appropriate at any stage during a management discussion – in order to bring together what has come out of the discussion up to a certain point.

A useful process for summarizing is to:

- *scan* (at a high level) the array of information which is available to you,
- identify which are the *most important* items,
- identify how these are *interdependent* with each other,
- identify the *patterns* emerging,
- define the *key insights* coming out of this, and
- ask: what is the 'so-what' from it?

The 'so-what' is a really important thing to consider, and this includes spelling out the implications of the summary. For example, should we be making any decisions as a result of it, or consider any other options which we have not looked at before? What are the possible consequences of this?

A more specific technique is that of following the 'weather forecast' model of making a presentation. This involves giving the 'so-what' of the presentation first, and then making a selective number of key points, making sure that you do draw out any linkages – and deliberately *leaving out some of the details*.

The latter point is the really hard thing to do.

So how do you ensure that you do not end up covering all of the details? To do this you definitely need to predetermine – in advance – which ones *you will leave out*.

The strategic option grid (see 'Option Generation', p. 249) is a really good way of presenting a strategic weather-forecast-style summary of a range of options, and of criteria for judging these options, together with scores of their relative attractiveness.

Killer takeaways include:

- tell them (your audience) of the message up-front, then tell it to them again (in detail), and then tell them it yet again (as a final, summarized reminder), and
- avoid going down into an inappropriate level of detail – or the rabbit hole – for any protracted period of time.

Summarizing fits well into many other skills, including:

- business cases (p. 79),
- business planning (p. 82),
- helicopter thinking (p. 40),
- presentations (making them) (p. 274),
- report writing (p. 227), and
- strategic thinking (p. 49).

Organizational Skills 8

CROSS-CULTURAL SKILLS

 ross-cultural skills are becoming an increasingly important element of the modern manager's skill-set. Cross-cultural skills are: 'Interpersonal skills which enable you to communicate, negotiate and manage across cultural boundaries.'
Cross-cultural skills involve a number of competencies:

- cultural knowledge – what do people do, behave like or think like in a particular culture,
- linguistic skills – the ability to understand, to speak, and to manage in another language, and
- behavioural adaptability – the ability to adapt your behaviour when dealing with a person of another cultural background. For instance, when dealing with a Japanese manager, allowing them a lot more time for reflection and decision-making.

To gain cross-cultural skills you may well need to spend periods of time either working with managers from other countries, or working in those countries themselves. This may be an attractive career move, besides enhancing your capability.

Cross-cultural skills are particularly appropriate when working on projects which span national boundaries, and also for alliances, acquisitions, and for selling in/to other countries.

Killer takeaways on cross-cultural skills include:

- Avoid saying or doing things which you are aware are no-nos – for example, in Latin countries it is normal to interrupt others, but in Anglo-Saxon countries this is considered to be rude. In Japan, it is also culturally quite normal to have pauses in conversations.
- Study cultural differences intensively before you ever conduct any business negotiation with managers from other countries.

Cross-cultural skills have a number of key links to many of the other skills, including:

- acquisitions integration (p. 107) (and negotiation),
- customer awareness (p. 57),
- empathizing (p. 182),
- global awareness (p. 38),
- influencing (p. 211),
- market research (p. 66) (outside natural boundaries), and
- product development (p. 69) (outside natural boundaries).

DELEGATION

elegation is a time-honoured skill for ensuring that you have a clearer focus on what you should be doing in your role. Delegation has the following pros:

- it helps you to practise what you should be doing/not doing,
- it can help develop your staff,
- it can take some pressure off you in your role, and
- it can help you to improve your skills – through concentrating on those areas which you are generally better at.

On the other hand, a con is that delegation shouldn't be used as an excuse for 'passing the parcel': just passing the work downwards so that you (as a manager) have a lower workload.

Delegation can be used in a variety of management situations, whether these are projects, or simply ongoing activities, such as writing a report, implementing a particular project, or perhaps a smaller task.

In delegating something it is crucial to position *why* something is to be delegated, for example:

- as an integral part of what they have as a fluid workload,
- it will help to alleviate your short-term workload or,
- it is part of a longer-term, planned job enlargement exercise,
- because the other person has better skills or resources to do it, either in less time, or to a higher quality standard, or both, and
- as a developmental exercise.

Delegation thus involves communication (and sometimes negotiation between) the delegator and the delegates rather than just dropping something on someone.

A killer takeaway for delegation is to place yourself in the delegates perspective: how will they see/feel about not only what you are trying to delegate, but also how, and when.

Delegation is linked to a number of other key skills including:

- action planning (p. 263),
- organization and people planning (p. 220),
- prioritization (p. 277),
- proactivity (p. 281),
- time management (p. 291), and
- training (p. 232).

INFLUENCING

I nfluencing is one of the most important management skills, following part of an interrelated cluster of skills including:

- negotiating,
- political awareness, and
- stakeholder management.

Influencing is possibly the skill you should be spending most time on, perhaps even more so than problem analysis. Influencing here doesn't have to be in your face, but can be quite subtle. In fact, we can define influencing as: 'A subtle process of helping others to see issues through a new perspective and, if necessary, to adjust their agendas so that you can meet the business, and perhaps your own personal goals, too.'

Clearly, where personal agendas intrude too much into the picture then this may become disadvantageous – as it is perceived that you are being manipulative. Also, there may well be ideas which you believe that the business needs, but this belief is not necessarily shared by others in the business. These agendas are both a blend of Personal And Strategic Agendas, which we can now call the 'PASTA' factors, to suggest that they are intermingled – and often in a messy way.

Besides the techniques contained elsewhere in the book which deal with influencing others, it is also interesting to look at the stakeholder network. This enables you to understand how one stakeholder's attitude links to another's, on a particular issue. The other thing which you should do is to understand how close any one stakeholder is to another – in terms of warmth of relationship. This will enable you to understand the various power blocs, or power zones, within the organization.

Another technique is to use the importance/urgency grid (see 'Prioritization', p. 277) in order to prioritize which stakeholders to try to win on board, and in which order.

Killer takeaways on influencing others include:

- Do a business case for action on a particular issue, to help persuade them.
- Seek to increase any dissatisfaction with the status quo, for example by asking 'what is putting up with this situation actually costing us?'
- Rather than try to impose an idea on others, sow the seeds of an idea in them.
- Ask the other stakeholder to say how they might be best influenced.

Other key skills closely associated with influencing include:

- business cases (p. 79),
- change management (p. 173),
- cross-cultural skills (p. 207),
- political awareness (p. 196),
- report writing (p. 227), and
- stakeholder management (p. 199).

INTERVIEWING

I

nterviewing is normally an interactive process which involves two sides coming together to explore the basis of a mutually beneficial agreement (in a job or other contractual context).

The above definition highlights that there is not necessarily an imbalance of power between the two sides. Strangely, in a recruitment context it is often the case that the interviewer would appear to have more power than the interviewee. But, whilst the interviewer has power over offering the job which he/she wants to fill, the interviewee has the negotiating power of their own options. So the conventional mindset of the interviewer of 'we sit here and ask the questions, then when we have finished we might just let you ask some – isn't that really nice of us?' is somewhat odd.

Interviews have a number of pros and cons. Their pros can be summarized as follows:

- they offer an opportunity for mutual exploration of options – by both parties, and
- they enable both sides to collect sufficient hard and soft data – to make a decision.

The cons are:

- they are often somewhat one-sided, and
- the 'definition of the situation' in an interview can give the applicant for a job the 'mindset' of 'I want to be successful in getting the job' or 'I would like to have an offer' – which can, in turn, lead to the mindset of 'I should accept it unless I see good reason not to'.

Outside the realm of work, interviews can, however, take other forms, such as the more neutral interview aimed at data collection. Here, the interviewer uses a series of questions to elicit data from the interviewee. In this situation there is much less of an obvious sense of inequality, and in fact the interviewee might well be of superior status than that of the interviewer.

Either way, the interviewer needs to have well-honed interpersonal skills, for example, listening, as we covered earlier.

Coming back now to job-related interviews, if you are an interviewer, you will need to:

- define what the objectives of appointing someone are – and its value-added,
- define your criteria (much as you would for an acquisition) of 'must-haves,' 'mustn't-haves' and 'nice-to-haves',
- define some key questions to help structure the interview, and also to focus your interview strategy, and
- define some criteria formally – to appraise the applicant.

If you are an interviewee:

- define your career strategy,
- define the objectives of your next job,
- define your criteria, for what you count as an attractive job,
- define (in advance) your key questions – for the interviewer,
- find out about your competitors/the sort of people who the other candidates are,
- evaluate your likely competitive advantage for the job,
- imagine the interviewer's criteria,
- imagine what questions you will be asked, and your answers/further questions,
- formulate your overall interview strategy,
- storytell how the interview is likely to go, and
- set down your ideal salary, your 'walk-away from' salary, and your 'must-have' terms and conditions etc.

Both sides can make use of:

- the strategic option grid (see 'Option Generation', p. 249),
- stakeholder analysis and agenda analysis,
- storytelling,
- the uncertainty/importance grid – for questioning your assumptions about the interviewee or the job, and
- wishbone analysis – for assessing the alignment factors for taking an appropriate job.

Interview questions can be closed (inviting the answer 'yes', 'no', or 'I don't know'), or they can be open (where the respondent can answer in any way they see fit). Make sure you ask enough open questions during an interview, to open up discussions.

Killer takeaways on interviews are:

- Have the 'out-of-body' experience – to help identify where the key stakeholders are likely to be positioned (and why), on the stakeholder analysis grid.
- If you are the interviewer, be prepared to ask questions like: 'looking back, what things have you done in a job which didn't work out, and what did you do to help avoid this, and what did you learn from the situation, and how it developed?'
- If you are the interviewee, be prepared to ask questions like: 'what would you say in your experience are the most difficult or frustrating things about working in this organization?' (a nice one to ask).
- Use the strategic skills to analyse the organization's current relative strength/weaknesses and its prospects.

Interviewing relates to a number of the softer skills, including:

- empathizing (p. 182),
- listening (p. 192),
- negotiating (p. 92),
- questioning (p. 258),
- self-awareness (p. 285),
- stakeholder management (p. 199),
- storytelling (p. 47),
- summarizing (p. 202), and
- time management (p. 291).

NETWORKING

Networking can be defined as: 'The activity of forging relationships with a divergent number of existing and potential stakeholders.'

Networking has a number of advantages:

- it enhances your ability to influence others, and strengthens your power base generally,
- it gives you improved data about the issues around you, and
- it may suggest specific opportunities for job moves, both within and outside the organization.

The only possible con of networking is that it does require some degree of time investment, some of which may be of uncertain benefit. But omitting to do sufficient networking can be a major cause of future regret. For instance one manager, a senior strategic planning director in a telecommunications company, was made redundant during an economic downtime. After the event, he reflected that:

> 'I used to network a lot, and know a lot of people in the telecoms industry. But given the day-to-day demands of the job, I neglected it for a few years, and thus found myself scratching around for warm contacts in looking for a job.'

Networking within your own organization is something which you can therefore be doing all the time – and this demands no real extra investment. To help cement relationships, it is often helpful to have lunch with people, to take advantage of annual company conferences, and to seize tactical opportunities given to you by chance encounters, such as a couple of minutes' chat at the end of a meeting. E-mail, too, offers fresh opportunities to build your network – as long as it is not abused through overuse!

In many ways, networking is a disproportionately important skill, and one that can be crucial to survival. One of our clients, an HR manager in another very large telecoms business, was able to resist pressures to move to an undesirable role, or to consider voluntary redundancy, by sheltering under a good relationship he had managed to nurture with the chairman of the group. This made it very difficult for middle-ranking sources of power to 'take him out'.

Another senior person, the partner of a major consulting firm, easily managed to survive an economic downturn through his ultra-strong network. Despite not having the most sophisticated skill-set technically, it was said that he was better networked internally than the head of the consultancy – and by a mile. There was therefore no question that he would survive tough times and (quite unusually in this kind of business) reach his natural retirement age which was a miracle in that organization.

Some killer takeaways on networking are:

- spend at least ten per cent of your time actively networking within your organization,
- use any external contact whatsoever to scan for possible job opportunities (for now, or for the future), and
- if you suspect for one second that there is a job-threatening restructuring around the corner, or that you will be acquired, sign up with some headhunters *now*, irrespective of whether you are/are not satisfied in your job.

Networking relates to a number of other key skills, including:

- e-mail management (p. 268),
- influencing (p. 211),
- learning (p. 271),
- proactivity (p. 281),
- self-development (p. 286), and
- stakeholder management (p. 199).

ORGANIZATIONAL DESIGN

O rganizational design is a black-hole and is not well understood by managers generally, and even more specifically, by HR managers. Organizational design can be defined as being: 'The process of developing organizational structures, skills, and styles in a cunning way, in order to achieve higher customer value and/or lower cost, and thus longer-term increase in shareholder value and in capability.'

This means that we are not looking merely at designing average organizations, but ones which will give us some distinctive and ground-breaking benefits. Also, we are designing the organization for some very specific and valuable goals, rather than on the basis of vague hunches that some organizational shape appears better.

The pros of proactive, organizational design are that:

- it can anticipate, rather than be reactive to further change, and
- it can help the organization have a logic beyond building it around the key, senior individuals that happen to be around at that time.

But a con can be that it becomes an exercise without a really clear vision, or becomes watered down to fit what is perceived to be manageable in the short run.

A useful process for organizational design is (Grundy and Brown 2003) to:

- define where you are now – in terms of organizational strengths and weaknesses, and your overall fit with the organizational environment,
- decide where you 'really-really-really want to be' in the future,
- look at the options for how you might get there – especially for the cunning plan,
- evaluate these options (using the strategic option grid – see 'Option Generation', p. 249), and

- put an economic value on your chosen option (however approximate).

Killer takeaways on organizational design thus include:

- do not get over-focused on where you are now – start your main line of thought by identifying where you 'really-really-really want to go' (or the 'Spice-Girl' approach), and
- you may even go as far as to have deliberate amnesia of 'where we are now' – forget the present organizational design and start from scratch.

Organizational design relates to a number of key skills areas including:

- change management (p. 173),
- direction setting (p. 179),
- forecasting (p. 156),
- option generation (p. 249),
- organization and people planning (p. 220),
- problem diagnosis (p. 254),
- recruiting (p. 225), and
- strategic thinking (p. 49).

Reference

Grundy, A.N. & Brown, L. (2003), *Value-Based HR Strategy*, Butterworth Heinnemann, Oxford.

ORGANIZATION AND PEOPLE PLANNING

O rganization and people planning is a skill closely related to that of the previous section on organizational design. More specifically, this is the process of defining competencies, staff levels, and development and recruitment activities in order to achieve your future organizational design.

The content of much of the plan thus drops out – in large part – from the previous section.

The pros of organization and people planning are that it:

- helps you to avoid sudden skills' bottlenecks (either in qualitative or in quantitative terms), and
- gives you (hopefully) enough lead time to cope with the demands of growth, or of change, or both of these.

The cons are that it can get taken too rigidly, resulting in the mere number-based production manpower plans that become irrelevant quickly, and which are unlikely to get acted upon.

A useful technique for organization and people planning is to do an extended form of gap analysis, called from–to (FT) analysis

To perform an FT analysis you need to carry out the following steps:

- what are you trying to shift? (the critical categories), and
- by how much are you trying to shift them? (the horizontal 'from' and 'to' shifts).

The key benefits of FT analysis are:

- it gives a clear and more complete vision of the extent of the potential difficulty that achieving that vision may give rise to,
- it can be used to actually monitor strategic change,

FROM ————————————————————→ TO

| | 1 | 2 | 3 | 4 | 5 |

Structures*

Goals*

Behaviours*

Cost base*

Responsiveness*

* You need to identify shifts relevant to you

Fig. 8.1 From–to (FT) analysis

- it is a very useful technique for communicating what needs to be done, or for exploring the implications and for getting greater buy-in, and
- as a spin-off, it is especially helpful in presenting business plans.

Killer takeaways on organization and people planning are:

- Do not confuse it with, or even call it, 'HR strategy,' as this almost inevitably will get confused with HR department, with a very real risk that it will become peripheral.
- Once you have done the from–to, you then need to work on the 'how?' which entails detailed project planning (and our 'how-how' technique).
- Always do a business case for why you should actually implement it, including its main value and cost drivers, and also the (approximate) net cash flows (where some estimation is feasible).

Key skills which are closely linked to organization and people planning include:

- change management (p. 173),
- direction setting (p. 179),
- organizational design (p. 218), and
- recruiting (p. 225).

PERFORMANCE APPRAISAL

P erformance appraisal is another important skill which many (even very experienced) managers struggle with. Performance appraisal is: 'The diagnosis of post performance in order a) to define past performance, b) to understand its causes, c) to identify and prioritize areas where improvement is both appropriate and feasible, d) to plan how this can be addressed, e) to discuss, prioritize and programme areas for longer-term development, and f) to set objectives (both short and long term) for the future.

Performance management thus *is not* just about remedial analysis, but is about understanding the causality of performance. This requires diagnosing where these causes are within/outside the control of the individual, and developing the support mechanisms for dealing with these areas. Finally, it necessitates thinking and also how that individual can be developed (e). Without any discussion of future developments, performance appraisal can turn into either a defensive display by the individual, or it can become a review that fails to really grapple with the underlying issues affecting an individual's performance.

The pros of performance appraisal are that it:

- is a forum for open and frank discussion about individual performance – and one which should be helpful to both parties,
- can help to turnaround weak or uneven performance, and
- gives the individual a much greater incentive to perform well (against mutually agreed objectives).

But there are potentially many cons:

- Feedback to the individual may not occur in the interim (between performance appraisals), so that he/she is suddenly confronted by a backlog of feedback which, if significantly negative, can produce either anger or even a decline in self-image. This can then result in a further decline in performance.

- If it is not well handled, this can help fuel an unfair dismissal case by the employee, later on.
- It can subsequently lead to disappointed staff leaving the company.

One of the authors once worked for BP and at his second annual appraisal he received an 'average' grade. Feeling that a) his performance had been better than average and b) that his work outside the UK – which had *not* been formally assessed – was generally good, and c) that this grading would rule him out from any career fast-track, he was understandably livid.

Subsequently, BP offered a number-crunching job in Malaysia instead of the corporate planning job the author aspired to, and at a time when his wife was doing a full-time degree course in Norwich. So, he decided that enough was enough, and went out for a self-appointed break. In five minutes he found himself in an accountancy personnel office in Moorgate, who booked him in to see a retailer in the West End for an interview that evening. He was offered a senior job with 20 per cent more money and took it that day.

Ironically, ten years later, he was back consulting at very senior levels at BP to help them change the culture and to become more flexible, and with more balanced appraisal methods like 360-degree feedback.

Taking up this specific theme next, performance appraisal can be linked to 360-degree feedback, where input about your perceived performance is drawn from your boss, your subordinates and your peers. Whilst being a very powerful process (and semi-anonymous) this can be a bit scary. Managers will often resist being put through this process – not surprisingly.

We have already seen how performance driver analysis ('Performance Analysis', p. 94) can be used to analyse performance at the business level. This technique can also be used in much the same way to diagnose an individual's performance. At a more micro level, fishbone analysis can then be used to diagnose a specific area of lower performance in more depth (see 'Problem Diagnosis', p. 254).

Killer takeaways on performance appraisal include:

- Set a maximum of three areas for major breakthroughs in performance, a larger number of more minor, continuous improvements, and at least *one* area for longer-term development.
- Find and exploit an organization with natural fit to your skills, style and mindset, rather than struggle fruitlessly with one that is obviously way out of fit.

Performance appraisal is linked to a number of other skills including:

- action planning (p. 263),
- coaching (p. 177),
- helicopter thinking (p. 40),
- motivating (p. 192),
- option generation (p. 249),
- organization and people planning (p. 220),
- performance analysis(p. 94),
- prioritization (p. 277),
- problem diagnosis (p. 254), and
- training (p. 232).

RECRUITING

R ecruiting is an important skill – whether it is for external or internal candidates for a job.

It may go without saying that you should first get really clear what the position in question is supposed to be for: what value will be added by the various activities within the role? Where the role is an existing position you now have the opportunity to redefine it, or the nature of the person you are looking for, or even whether you need to consider a part-timer, or outsourcing. Where it is a new role your scope for freedom of role definition is obvious.

Recruitment may thus be a much more fluid task than you may have supposed.

It is a healthy discipline, too, to write a short business case for the role: what is the value (to the business) of the role's outputs? Will additional sales be generated as a result of the role (directly or indirectly)? Or will costs be saved, or will any value, which would otherwise have been destroyed, now be protected?

The next step is to determine your criteria for the role, together with some view of how important these criteria are. Appointing someone to a role is a key strategy, so it is crucial to do a strategic comparison of how different candidates stack up. Also, it can be used to set a benchmark for making any kind of appointment at all, rather than just to simply fill the vacancy from available candidates.

The strategic option grid (see 'Option Generation', p. 249) can be used either as it stands, or in a tailored form, to carry out the analysis. This more generic approach contains some real benefits as follows:

- through its focusing on strategic attractiveness it can cover the longer term and not just the shorter term,
- financial attractiveness helps incorporate the salary costs, the costs of training the individual, the lead time to their being fully effective etc.,

- some candidates may be more/less difficult to integrate into the organization: hence, implementation difficulty is helpful too,
- risk and uncertainty analysis is a useful tool for weeding out suspicious candidates, and
- stakeholder acceptability helps to incorporate potential political fit with the organization – and explicitly.

Killer takeaways for recruitment include:

- Tell scenario stories about how the individual is likely to perform in that role, as he/she meets its demands as they come up, and change over time in the future.
- Do a wishbone analysis (see 'Product Development', p. 69) for how their good performance needs to be supported by all the support factors lining up – including proper induction, coaching, and through appropriate allocation of tasks etc.

Recruitment thus relates to a number of skills:

- business cases (p. 79),
- interviewing (p. 213),
- option generation (p. 249),
- organizational designs (p. 218),
- organization and people planning (p. 220),
- risk and uncertainty analysis (p. 44),
- storytelling (p. 47),
- strategic thinking (p. 49), and
- training (p. 232).

REPORT WRITING

eport writing is a skill that is rapidly being forgotten by Power-Point junkies, and those who now think primarily in bullet points. But report writing is an excellent way of developing your ideas, and of soliciting others' input on them. One of the major benefits of doing an MBA is that it sharpens these skills considerably.

The benefits of writing a short report (rather than just sending an e-mail, or doing a presentation) are that it:

- allows you to collect and interpret some data,
- helps ensure appropriate issue/problem definition,
- develops the ideas, especially options,
- gives you space to draw out the implications, and
- provides an opportunity to ask some key questions.

A useful format is to call it a 'position paper'. Here, the idea is not necessarily to reach conclusions, but to develop and share ideas, judgements and opinions, before making or proposing a decision. A position paper can be anything between 3–5 pages and can be circulated around the various stakeholders to get their input, and even rewording, electronically.

Typically a position paper reduces the overall time to write a business plan (for instance) by around 50 per cent – or more – and can double the buy-in of key stakeholders.

Whatever the topic, fishbone analysis (see 'Problem Diagnosis', p. 254) is an invaluable technique to begin with (and/or gap analysis). Another essential technique is the strategic option grid (see 'Option Generation', p. 249), for evaluation/prioritization of possible solutions. The strategic option grid is also helpful for structuring any position paper, with a core section then being able to work option-by-option through the grid, focusing on its most important boxes in this particular context.

A really well written report can also help to position you as having high potential and often in a more immediate way than giving input at meetings.

Killer takeaways include:

- What is the one big thing you have missed in your position paper?
- Have the out-of-body experience of how readers will see it (and do a stakeholder analysis – see 'Stakeholder Management', p. 199).
- List some key questions for either further discussion or to steer data gathering.

Report writing is linked to:

- helicopter thinking (p. 40),
- option generation (p. 249),
- prioritization (p. 277),
- problem diagnosis (p. 254),
- summarizing (p. 202), and
- strategic thinking (p. 49).

TEAMWORKING

Teamworking is the process of interacting in a group in order to generate value in an organization. Teams can meet regularly, or be more 'virtual' in nature.

The advantages of teams are that:

- they can create more ideas (than individuals alone),
- they can look at a variety of perspectives, and
- they can get faster buy-in.

The possible drawbacks of teams are that:

- they demand a lot of co-ordination,
- they are expensive – gathering together a group of individuals who are only adding a lot of value part of the time is expensive,
- they can actually slow things down,
- they can become bureaucratic, political, or both,
- they can take a lot of time and investment to ensure that they work effectively, and
- there may be a narrowing of views to create a sense of consensus – sometimes known as groupthink – where no one is prepared to challenge the prevailing view.

When teams are created it is said that they tend to go through three key phases before they become fully effective:

- forming.
- storming, and
- performing.

The storming phase suggests that they often underperform as the key individuals within them become adjusted to one another, and to the group setting and dynamics. Team building is a process of accelerating these adjustments, typically linking the form of an offsite or onsite event to:

- debate issues and priorities,
- come up with a way of working (their rules of engagement),
- determine a vision,
- decide on individual roles, and
- determine its value added.

A diagnostic for understanding what makes a performing team came out of the authors' research (Grundy 1998 – see Fig. 8.2).

Besides the conventional stuff about getting a balanced team mix (perhaps using Belbin-type role diagnosis: like 'plant', 'shaper', 'chairperson', 'finisher', 'resource investigator') this system of strategic team behaviour also stresses:

- task definition (what is the team going to do?),
- outputs (and their value),
- team dynamics, and
- analytical process, for instance, the strategic option grid or fishbone analysis).

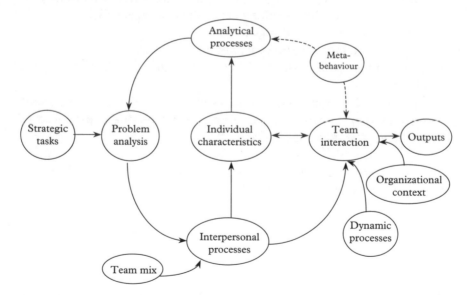

Fig. 8.2 The system of strategic behaviour

Teamworking killer takeaways include:

- Decide which 'p' behaviours you do not wish to have – within the team and in advance – including being personal, political, picky, pedantic, overprotective etc.
- Monitor the value-over-time curve of the team's output – both before, during and after the event.
- Where a team is over five people in strength, break into sub-teams to work on sub-tasks and then come back together again, to share and compare outputs.
- Determine what team role you are normally best at (for example 'plant', 'shaper' etc., and then practise some of the other team roles).

Teamworking is linked to a number of key skills, including:

- direction setting (p. 249),
- facilitation (p. 249),
- helicopter thinking (p. 249),
- option generation (p. 249),
- organizational design (p. 249),
- organization and people planning (p. 249),
- problem diagnosis (p. 249),
- recruiting (p. 249), and
- value management (p. 249).

Reference

Grundy, A.N. (1998) *Strategic Behaviour*, FT Publishing, London.

TRAINING

Training is the process of developing the skills of staff in order to define value for the organization. Training can be conducted both on and off the job.

The pros of off-the-job training are that it can:

- get staff up to speed and in an accelerated time period,
- combine analytical with behavioural learning, even with mindset and cultural change, and
- be very motivating.

The cons of off-the-job training are that:

- learning often decays – and quite quickly, if it is not put into action quickly, and also reinforced, and
- training events are expensive, not merely in terms of their direct cost, but also in terms of the investment in managers' time, which could have been used for other productive work.

Effective training should therefore include:

- A thorough training-needs analysis – to understand the key skills gaps, to prioritize their importance, and to target who will benefit from the training (fishbone analysis can be very helpful here to diagnose apparent skills deficiencies).
- Assessment of the options for delivering the training: on-the-job/ off-the-job, tailored-versus-public programmes, coaching etc. (see Grundy & Brown 2003).
- Sourcing/resourcing these solutions.
- Targeting their value.
- Evaluation of their effectiveness.
- Reinforcement of their effects.

A manager does not have a passive role in training – it is not just something for the HR department to do. He/she should:

- be integrally involved in any kind of training-needs analysis, and
- be actively involved in on-the-job and off-the-job training, and not just in a symbolic capacity.

Killer takeaways on training include:

- Benchmark and learn from what kinds of training have worked most effectively by looking elsewhere – both inside and outside your company, and elsewhere within and even outside your industry.
- To help evaluate the value of training, work backwards from the targeted business value (in a real-life business situation) which might arise from different behaviours. (This is sometimes called 'critical incident analysis' where a particular incident which is the product of learning adds value.)

Training is linked to many skills areas, including:

- coaching (p. 177),
- organization and people planning (p. 220), and
- teamworking (p. 229).

Reference

Grundy, A.N. & Brown, L. (2003) *Developing the Individual*, Capstone Publishing, Oxford.

Problem-solving Skills 9

ALIEN THINKING

O ne of the central ways of beginning to challenge our ideas is to practice alien thinking. In other words, imagine that you have, as it were, just landed from another planet, and are thus totally free from normal preconceptions. Alien thinking of this kind has a number of key benefits:

- it puts managers into a much more creative space, allowing them to challenge their mindsets, and
- it helps you to take not just a helicopter thinking perspective, but a global perspective also.

As an example of alien thinking, one of the authors was asked to run some alien awaydays for a major bank in Ireland. On arriving he said: 'Thank you very much for inviting me to your alien day. I have a confession to make: I actually *am* an alien. And what I would say is that in 22 years on your planet Earth I have never been treated individually by a bank. Look at all these cards! (scattering his debit and credit cards on the client's carpet). Every time I have had problems with a bank, I have never been dealt with on an individual basis. So, my message to you is: I want to be treated as an individual/human being.'

The results of this insight were then used to reprioritize the bank's marketing strategy and also to become the centrepiece of their advertising campaign on Irish TV.

Alien thinking can be used in a variety of contexts, particularly for strategy development or even for organizational design, or restructuring, or for cost management.

A killer takeaway is to imagine that your workshop is an end-of-the-world workshop: that the world will be ended by alien attack – and, in say three hours, that you have to come up with a solution to your chosen management problem to prevent this from happening. This gives you an incisive edge to move on, and to challenge when dealing with issues.

Alien thinking can be linked to a number of other key business skills, including:

- cost management (p. 146),
- helicopter thinking (p. 40),
- organizational design (p. 218),
- product development (p. 69), and
- strategic thinking (p. 49).

BRAINSTORMING

Brainstorming is a technique associated with writer and thinker Edward de Bono. It refers to the process of idea generation – but where these ideas are generated in free-flow and without evaluation or, especially, criticism.

The pros of brainstorming are that it:

- can generate a very large number of ideas – very quickly,
- it generates a lot of fun and energy, and
- some ideas then generate new ideas in a naturally flowing sequence of thought.

The cons of brainstorming are that it:

- can produce a lot of ideas which are not of very high quality, and
- requires a lot of subsequent clearing up afterwards, to sort out the good ideas from the not-so-good.

Brainstorming needs to be done by generating ideas as a free stream – rather like in psychotherapy, through the association of ideas. These are often written on Post-its®, which can then be put into categories and prioritized (see techniques in 'Prioritization', p. 277). Another technique is to put disparate ideas together as a group, to see if – in an unlikely combination – they suggest new options and ideas. When brainstorming, it is useful to find a group of managers who have at least some degree of creativity, otherwise the process can run dry.

Brainstorming has evolved over the years and there are very many approaches to it – probably as many as there are consultants who have used, and tailored, the process. In the section on 'Option Generation' (p. 249) we explore the 'optopus' which contains eight generic lines of enquiry – such as: which customer segments can we address? – providing not only a stimulus for creating an idea in a particular direction, but also putting a little bit more structure into the process.

Also, in the forthcoming section on creativity we look at a number of questions that will prompt you to be more creative.

Killer takeaways on brainstorming include:

- Don't do brainstorming without at least some ideas about how you will (later on) screen or prioritize these ideas.
- Try to establish a number of possible lines of enquiry first. What are the likely rich sources of ideas (for example, ideas from customers, ideas drawn from how something works really well in other industries, etc.)?
- You really *must* have a facilitator for this (whether internal or external), otherwise you are very likely to end up with an unproductive and chaotic mess.

Brainstorming links to:

- creativity (p. 245),
- facilitation (p. 186),
- imagination (p. 247),
- option generation (p. 249), and
- prioritization (p. 277).

BUILDING

uilding is a problem-solving process that entails offering constructive suggestions in order to develop ideas – rather than to test them. Building is a very positive process and skill, not only because it can help turn an average set of ideas into a cunning plan, but also because it can fill gaps in existing thinking. This can help to add real value to any kind of strategic or more tactical business review, rather than it being primarily an exercise in simply picking something apart.

Building on what already exists can be done in a number of ways:

- by suggesting how an option can be made better,
- by suggesting a new combination of existing ideas (as an option),
- through putting forward an entirely new option,
- by suggesting a different way of implementing a particular option, and
- by proposing which key stakeholders might now be influenced – when, how and by whom.

Building can be built into your team-building process. It is also a key ingredient in all strategic business reviews or during any kind of creative/innovative session.

Building's sister skill is 'challenging'. Both can be used more or less together. In some companies the order is normally 'challenge and build', but in our view a more constructive approach frequently is to 'build and (then) challenge', rather than vice versa.

Some killer takeaways on building are:

- Focus first on what is good about an idea, rather than starting with what is wrong with it.
- See if you can make a good idea even better. (But return respect for the ownership of the original idea – so that it is clear that your own

idea doesn't supersede the old one, but it just makes it even more
superior.)
- Even if you can't come up with a brilliant idea yourself ask managers
to see if they can come up with a cunning plan themselves.

Building relates to a number of other key skills, including:

- creativity (p. 245),
- helicopter thinking (p. 40),
- imagination (p. 247),
- influencing (p. 211),
- option generation (p. 249),
- strategic thinking (p. 49),
- storytelling (p. 47), and
- teamworking (p. 229).

CHALLENGING

C hallenging is the sister skill to building (p. 241). Challenging involves testing the robustness of specific proposals, or options, or of the underlying assumptions. Challenging works best when it is accompanied by building – to avoid becoming too destructive a process.

Examples of challenging include asking nine key questions to check out:

1   Do we have any key objectives, and do these make sense with one another?
2   Are the big objectives mutually consistent?
3   Do the options actually meet our key objectives?
4   Are the options really as attractive as we think they are?
5   Will we really be able to implement them as easily as we think we can?
6   What are the key downsides to our ideas, and what is their potential impact?
7   When we did this type of thing last time (and it did not work out), why was this, and what makes us think that it will be different this time?
8   What is the opportunity cost of actually going ahead with this idea?
9   What is the one big thing which we might have missed?

Obviously these questions are quite easy and powerful as a set, and it is easy to mount a barrage which will destroy ideas at their formative stage. This is *not* the purpose of challenging; it should be accompanied simultaneously by the building process. You might say, for example:

'I am not sure that this proposal will be able to cope with the economic slowdown as it is, but if we were to package it differently, and sell it a different way – perhaps through a different distribution channel – this might make it a success.'

The main analytical techniques for challenging include:

- the strategic option grid (see 'Option Generation', p. 249), and
- the uncertainty grid (see 'Risk and Uncertainty Analysis', p. 44).

Killer takeaways on challenging include:

- Always avoid making this appear to be either a direct or indirect personal attack on someone.
- Make sure that you practise the out-of-body experience – if you were the other party, how would you feel if you were subjected to this kind of challenge?
- Make 'build and challenge' a regular part of your management process.

Challenging relates to a number of key skills, including:

- building (p. 241),
- business cases (p. 79),
- empathizing (p. 182),
- problem diagnosis (p. 254) (what might go wrong and why),
- questioning (p. 258),
- risk and uncertainty analysis (p. 44),
- stakeholder management (p. 199), and
- storytelling (p. 47).

CREATIVITY

C reativity is a very important area for managers to develop. Many managers do not see themselves as being particularly creative. Also, the nature of managerial work is often such that managers perceive there to be relatively little scope to be truly creative. Many are trapped in a reactive cycle of responding to fairly random, short-term needs, and see little real chance to break out into some more free-thinking space.

The penalty, however, for not developing your creativity is that you are destined to be trapped in an ongoing cycle of reactiveness.

The pros of being creative are:

- you can solve problems far more easily, and effectively,
- it gives you a sense of freedom, and greater energy, generally, and
- it is the seed of most forms of competitive advantage.

A con of being creative is that you can become intoxicated by your own ideas, but then cannot be bothered to implement them as this is less stimulating than your original creative process.

Almost all management situations are ones in which you can exercise at least some degree of creativity. For instance, if you hold regular meetings with your team, what are the options for achieving twice value-added as much, in half the time? For instance should you abandon your normal seats and opt for high stools – as if you are at a bar (and thus you are deliberately less comfortable), to help give a greater sense of urgency? Or should you, like Stelios of Easygroup, get rid of all chairs entirely? And, for every issue, should you have managers come prepared to any meeting with the following questions?

- Why is it a problem/or an issue?
- What are the options for solving it?
- How attractive and difficult are these options?

- What are the implications of the proposed solution for this issue?
- Who now needs to be won over and/or do what?

In which case, you should be able to (easily) half the time of any normal meeting – indeed, your agenda should shrink to focus on the absolutely essential.

Creativity is not easily bottled as a commodity, nor are there set-piece solutions for stimulating it (such as conventional brainstorming) which can suddenly make everyone double their creativity. Nevertheless, by adapting a *questioning* approach to all issues one can go a long way towards becoming more creative, for example:

- Use the alien approach proactively (see 'Alien Thinking', p. 237). What would a new arrival on our planet make of a particular situation?
- Have a strategic amnesty so that here you forget anything that has gone wrong in the past (the advantage being that you are more able to think freely about options).
- Imagine that you have never dealt with this issue before or that this is your first day in your job, or your company, or even in your industry.
- Zero-base your resources – imagine that there are no resources allocated. If you were starting from scratch what resources would you really like to deploy?
- Search for the cunning plan, this is a simple but innovative way of achieving your goal with least cost, time and difficulty.
- Define your vision and then work backwards from 'what you really-really-really want' (the 'Spice-Girl strategy') to arrive at your plan.
- Practise the 'joy of constraints'. If someone says 'we can't do this', then get more excited (in finding a possible solution) rather than less.

Creativity links to a number of our other skills, including:

- direction setting (p. 179),
- energizing (p. 184),
- facilitation (p. 186),
- helicopter thinking (p. 40),
- imagination (p. 247),
- option generation (p. 249),
- problem diagnosis (p. 254),
- questioning (p. 258),
- storytelling (p. 47), and
- strategic thinking (p. 49).

IMAGINATION

I magination is inextricably linked to creativity. Imagination is about thinking how things could be different, from the status quo, either now or in the future. The benefits of imagination are that it allows you to build on *and* challenge current thoughts and approaches. It also helps you to generate new options, and provides a basis for storytelling about the future.

The only real disadvantages of imagination is that it sometimes goes into runaway mode – and is then not grounded in realistic action. Alternatively it may conjure pictures of the future so terrible that you become frozen in a state of anxiety.

Imagination is mostly highly productive. In competitive strategy you can, for instance, imagine breaking the current rules of the game. Indeed, the authors' book *Be Your Own Strategy Consultant* (2002) suggests that imagination:

- gives back the sense of control (over strategy) to the client,
- demystifies strategy, thus helping grow the market, and
- means that clients can receive the benefits associated with external strategy advice – without having the embarrassment (and cost) of letting swarms of strategy consultants into their company.

Killer takeaways on imagination are:

- Imagine the future and how you are successful in it, and what are the specific battle conditions – then work backwards to identify your strategy or your tactics
- The future is said to be the 'place where we will spend the rest of our lives' – so why not invest in thinking about it a bit?
- Imagine *how* you would do something if you were someone else – another competitor, a new entrant, or a famous turnaround manager like Sir John Harvey Jones.

Imagination thus has a number of potential ingredients:

- imagining the future (and in some detail) and then working backwards to how you got there,
- deconstructing your business model and then reassembling this with new ingredients, and
- imagining you are able to compete on a much bigger, possibly global, scale (as in the above example from *Be Your Own Strategy Consultant*).

Imagination is closely linked with:

- creativity (p. 245),
- helicopter thinking (p. 40),
- option generation (p. 249), and
- strategic thinking (p. 49).

OPTION GENERATION

O ption generation is a process for developing and evaluating key options. The advantages of more systematic option generation are that it ensures that a wider (and more complete) range of solutions will be considered.

Options fall into a number of key variables, including:

- *what* you are going to do,
- *how* you are going to do it,
- *when* you are going to do it, and
- *who* is going to do it.

Each one of these options can be explored using the strategic option grid, which will be explored below (Figs 9.2 and 9.3).

But before we look at this, let us take a look at *how* we can generate options. Here we use the 'optopus', which contains eight avenues to develop (competitive) strategy options with (see Fig. 9.1). (Obviously this needs tailoring if we are looking at an internal strategy.) These generic 'lines of enquiry' can be then used to create 'mix and match' options.

For example, a grocery home-shopping business could focus on:

- the Queen (and the royal family),
- delivery to stately/country homes,
- delivery by Discovery, 4WD,
- royal produce, including game, cheese, fine wines and shotgun ammunition, and
- alliances with exclusive suppliers.

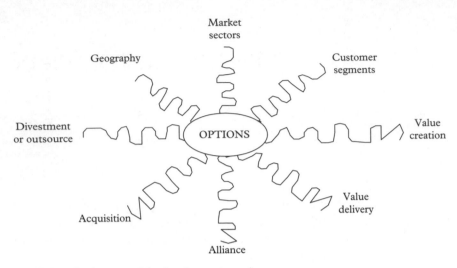

Fig. 9.1 The 'optopus' (or 'option octopus)

Another technique for generating and evaluating options is the strategic option grid (see Fig. 9.2). This consists of five key criteria:

- strategic attractiveness,
- financial attractiveness,
- implementation difficulty,
- uncertainty and risk, and
- stakeholder acceptability.

OPTIONS / CRITERIA	OPTION 1	OPTION 2	OPTION 3	OPTION 4
STRATEGIC ATTRACTIVENESS				
FINANCIAL ATTRACTIVENESS*				
IMPLEMENTATION DIFFICULTY				
UNCERTAINTY AND RISK				
ACCEPTABILITY (TO STAKEHOLDERS)				

* Benefits less costs, - net cash flows relative to investment

Fig. 9.2 Strategic option grid

This is then scored to reflect whether it is:

- highly attractive (★★★),
- moderately attractive (★★), or
- low attractiveness (★).

Half ticks are possible, too.

For implementation difficulty, three ticks represents 'low difficulty' and one tick is 'very difficult'. Also, for uncertainty and risk, three ticks reflects low uncertainty and risk, and one tick is high uncertainty and risk.

A completed grid is now shown in Fig. 9.3.

Strategic attractiveness can be defined according to a number of factors including:

- market growth (present),
- market volatility,
- competitive intensity,
- future market growth,
- fit with own capability,
- fit to own brand,
- your likely edge over competitors,
- the scale of the opportunity, and
- degree of focus, or possible dilution of one's own strategy.

	Closure 1	Cost cutting 2	Price rises 3	Options 2 & 3 plus more funding 4
Strategic attractiveness	★★★	★	★★	★★★
Financial attractiveness	★★	★★	★★★	★★★
Implementation difficulty	★	★★	★	★★
Uncertainty and risk	★	★★	★	★★
Stakeholder acceptability	★	★★	★	★★★
Total score	8	9	8	13

Fig. 9.3 Strategic option grid for railway telephone enquiry system

Financial attractiveness can be defined as 'Value less costs, relative to investment.' Implementation difficulty is the sum of the difficulty over time to achieve a particular strategic and financial result. Uncertainty and risk reflects the option's relative volatility and vulnerability. Stakeholder acceptability is the weighted average picture gained by looking at relative stakeholder support versus influence (see also 'Stakeholder Management', p. 199).

Each of the boxes on the strategic option grid can then be subjected to more detailed analysis and data collection. Also, each option's overall scores are only as good as your cunning plan. Once data collection (and sensitivity analysis) has been conducted, you can now refine, and finalize the scores.

The grid can be used for:

- acquisitions
- alliances,
- organic strategies,
- project management,
- restructurings, and
- evaluating your career options.

There are a number of potential ways of using the strategic option grid. First, one can use it on a stand-alone basis to sort out high-level options. These might be options for a) what to do where these options are quite separate, b) what to do when there are a variety of routes to achieve the same goal, and c) different implementations. Where options for 'different things we can do' are positioned across the top of the grid, effectively the 'options for how to do it' create a third dimension which is behind the page. All (ultimately) need exploring, and may require a number of more detailed grids to look at implementation options.

Secondly, the grid can be used alongside the more detailed techniques contained in the rest of this book. This can be done in two orders, either a) *after* using the more detailed techniques (GE grid, uncertainty grid etc.), and perhaps also after some selected data collection, or b) to check out judgements on one specific option after you have done your higher-level analysis.

The advantage of not doing a very detailed analysis up front is that more options can be thought through, and also this will minimize premature commitment to a specific option. (Typically, when data is collected, commitment to a specific course of action tends to increase.) The disadvantage of the more high-level approach is that in the wrong hands

– which analyses only one main option in depth – the broader analysis of all options might be subjective.

Whilst the strategic option grid is a potent technique for group or for individual decision making, it needs some caution particularly with regard to the following:

- In assessing strategic attractiveness, users will often rate highly simply because they are attracted to the opportunity or decision. In reality, however, the option may be unattractive due to its unfavourable market attractiveness, or its likely competitive position, or both.
- Financial attractiveness may rate low on the scale simply because the decision requires longer-term investment. But, provided that future returns are good, there may be grounds for taking a more positive judgement.
- Implementation difficulty may be underestimated as only the early stage of implementation is thought through.
- Risk and uncertainty – again, key uncertainties may not be uncovered, resulting in a bias to optimism. This requires further analysis using the uncertainty grid.
- Stakeholder and acceptability – unless the positions of the various key stakeholders (now and in the future) have been thought through in detail, then the view taken might be either under- or over-optimistic.

Killer takeaways include:

- use the strategic option grid for your future career options, and
- use it in everyday personal life – for example for moving house, moving in with a new partner, getting married etc. – it is great practice and yields some fantastic spin-offs.

Option generation is a crucial skill, with links to:

- all the strategy skills (p. 13ff),
- organizational design (p. 218), and
- problem diagnosis (p. 254).

PROBLEM DIAGNOSIS

roblem diagnosis is an area where managers can add a lot of value, either at the strategic or at the tactical level.

The pros of systematic problem diagnosis are:

- you can treat the root causes of problems, rather than grappling with their symptoms, and
- besides current problem-solving, you can use it to *anticipate*, and to head off, *future* problems, hence becoming more proactive.

Possible cons of problem diagnosis are that:

- you can lose sight of the bigger picture, by analysing in too great a depth, and
- you can forget to generate options which might reframe the problem.

Problem diagnosis can be addressed by using fishbone analysis, as follows.

Fishbone analysis is a very quick and easy way of going behind the more immediate definition of the problem or opportunity. For instance, Fig. 9.4 illustrates why strategy is frequently not well implemented. This can be due to a variety of reasons, or underlying root causes. These include, for example, having too abstract a strategic vision, not fully thinking through implementation, or through having too many unprioritized projects.

There are some important guidelines for using fishbone analysis. The dos are:

- Identify the symptom of the cause and position it on the right-hand side. Where there are a number of possible symptoms you might need to analyse several problems (and thus draw up several fish-

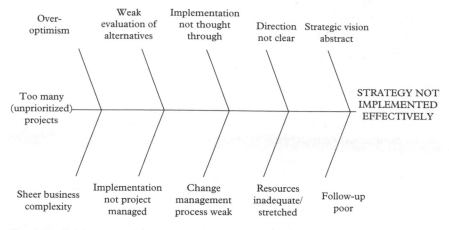

Fig. 9.4 Fishbone analysis

bones). Or, you may need to summarize a number of issues into a single, overarching fishbone.

- Make sure that the root causes are the real root causes. If you can still ask the question 'why?' then you are still dealing with the symptom.
- Use your common sense to understand at what point you should cease going back up the causal chain. Thus a 'lack of leadership skills' for most purposes is a satisfactory root cause rather than going back to 'the Board appointed the wrong leader' or 'there were no really suitable candidates'. (You do not need to go back to the dawn of time to necessarily scope and diagnose a problem.)

The don'ts are:

- Don't worry about whether the fishbone causes should go vertically or downwards – there is no special priority in where they are positioned – they are all equivalent. Most fishbones are more complete if they are drawn up in a creative flow, rather than in some pre-structured manner. If you do want to prioritize the fishbone, write the root causes on Post-its® and then move them around, perhaps in order of priority of attractiveness, or difficulty, or your degree of influence, over them.
- Don't clutter up the analysis with sub-bones off a main fishbone on the very same sheet of paper. This produces a visually complex, messy, and hard-to-interpret picture. Where appropriate, do the analysis of a particular mini-fishbone for a particular cause on a separate page.

- Don't forget to consider the external causes as well as the internal root causes, and also the tangible versus the less tangible causes of the original symptom.

The key benefits of fishbone analysis are that it:

- Helps diagnose a problem in much greater depth, helping to scope strategic issues much more effectively.
- Usually goes halfway (at least) towards suggesting solutions.
- Reduces the tendency for managers to talk about the same issues over and over again – using different words just creates greater confusion and slows progress significantly.
- Communicates the scope and the key reasons for the problem in a politically neutral way – it is an essential technique for managing upwards.
- Provides a means of linking strategic analysis with implementation (for example, by taking gaps within a competitor profile and using a fishbone to tease out the detailed causes which need to be addressed).
- Allows you to go freely up and down levels of analysis without getting irretrievably lost down the rabbit holes.

Its potential downsides are that:

- It can reinforce the 'it is a problem' mindset.
- Managers do tend to restrict themselves to solving the causes of the problem with fishbone analysis, rather than examining where they might be (the cunning plan).
- Unless a fishbone is prioritized (which we will see later), it only takes you a limited way forward.

Killer takeaways are:

- use fishbone analysis to diagnose *why* you find time management a problem,
- it is a life-saver when dealing with any kind of relationship problem in management, and
- it should also be used in order to diagnose (in detail) the cause of some factor restricting performance.

Problem diagnosis is linked especially to:

- change management (p. 173) (ask: why should you do it?),
- cost management (p. 146) (ask: why are costs too high?),
- performance analysis (p. 94),
- performance appraisal (p. 222),
- proactivity (p. 281),
- questioning (p. 58) (ask: why is something a problem?),
- storytelling (p. 47) (about how an event in the future might crystallize), and
- time management (p. 291).

QUESTIONING

uestioning is about asking the right questions in order to open up new possibilities, to help identify gaps, and to generally challenge mindsets. Questioning has a number of key advantages:

- it gets people to think about an issue a lot harder than normal,
- it helps generate a much wider range of options, and
- it helps to challenge, and ultimately to get around, perceived constraints.

But questioning can have some key disadvantages:

- it can be uncomfortable and threatening to be on the receiving end of it, especially if it is very direct, and
- it can be unhelpful – if the other party thinks that *you already know the answer to the question* (which you may, or may not), they may feel stupid, and become defensive.

But having said that, questioning is a highly value-added process, which can help you to justify your (hopefully) premium salary as a manager. Some key, challenging questions to focus your questioning are:

- What business are we really in?
- Why do we do things this way?
- Why is this issue really a problem?
- What are the options for doing this?
- What is the opportunity cost of doing this?
- What are the longer-term implications of doing this?
- What is the business case for doing this?

Killer takeaways include:

- When someone asked you to do something which you feel is inappropriate you can ask the following ten questions.
  - What is the objective?
  - What other options exist for doing it?
  - How attractive is this really going to be?
  - How difficult is this going to be?
  - How uncertain is this going to be?
  - Am I the best person to do this really well?
  - What is the cost of me not doing other things (now) – if I do this?
  - What is the cost of me not being able to do other, new things in the future?
  - What does the business case look like for doing this?
  - What stakeholder support will we have for doing this?

Questioning is thus very closely related to:

- all of the strategy skills (p. 13ff),
- business cases (p. 79),
- business planning (p. 82),
- challenging (p. 243),
- direction setting (p. 179),
- facilitation (p. 186),
- problem diagnosis (p. 254),
- prioritization (p. 277), and
- time management (p. 291) (for example, ask yourself why does this take so long/why are we doing it?)

Self-management Skills

10

ACTION PLANNING

ction planning is the systematic breakdown of activities that will be both necessary and sufficient to achieve my goal. Action planning is essential in order to turn ideas (whether tactical or strategic) into action. Action planning's only real downside is that it often focuses too much on goals, and not enough on the 'how'.

Action planning can be applied to issues at the:

- corporate plan level,
- business plan level,
- departmental plan level,
- project plan level, and
- individual level (either day-to-day, or developmental).

Action planning can be supported by a number of key techniques:

- work breakdown analysis,
- attractiveness/implementation difficulty (AID) analysis,
- the urgency/importance grid (see 'Prioritization', p. 277),
- Gantt chart analysis (effectively a series of bar diagrams for breaking down activities over time), and
- critical path analysis (plotting activities as a networked sequence of activities in order to understand the longest path through the activities – and thus to identify that route which, if delayed at all, will delay the entire project).

Killer takeaways are:

- What one key activity (which you have omitted) is needed to deliver the necessary result?
- Understand, and balance the trade-off between desired result, time, and cost, throughout your action planning.

Action planning is closely related to:

BEING INTERVIEWED

We have already covered many aspects of the interview process in the section on 'Interviewing' (p. 213) – so this will be a relatively short section.

Being interviewed successfully is all about letting your interviewers believe that *they* are in control (most of the time) when really it is *you* who are in control most of the time.

This demands:

- Anticipating the questions you may be asked (in advance, and in detail).
- Drawing up your draft answers, and also your counter-questions.
- Having a clear list of your own questions and ensuring that you have about a third of the back end of the interview to ask them – this gives you a lot more of the ball, as it were.
- Performing your stakeholder analysis (and your out-of-body experience) of the other stakeholders in advance.
- Being prepared to ask them at some stage, 'what are your criteria for making a decision about this?' and also, potentially 'who is going to be involved in the decision-making process?' and finally, 'what are your (likely) timescales for making a decision?'

Being interviewed relates to:

- challenging (p. 243),
- influencing (p. 211),
- proactivity (p. 281),
- questioning (p. 258),
- stakeholder management (p. 199), and
- storytelling (p. 47).

DRIVE

rive is an essential ingredient of a prospective senior manager. We define drive as: 'Your determination to deliver results and to succeed, and not to be off put by any frustrations and set-backs.'

The pros of drive are that:

- it can sustain you through unforeseen disruption and difficulties,
- it can help you to seek ways around obstacles, and
- it can help you in your task of motivating and energizing others.

Its potential cons are that:

- It can cause you to pursue a goal blindly, and prevent you from thinking about the other options, or even the cunning plan.
- It can turn off people around you, who might not share your drive – and need to be allowed a little more time and space to buy into it.
- It can burn you out unless you can learn to turn it down – albeit temporarily – to restore your energy.

Drive isn't something that analytical techniques can help you with directly, because it is a personal attribute. However, you can use fishbone analysis to reflect on why you might be losing drive – and begin to think of ways of restoring it.

A killer takeaway for drive is that if you need a lot or more of it – temporarily – then, as you are going off to a meeting, play in your head the theme tune to *Mission Impossible*.

Drive relates to a number of key business skills, including:

- action planning (p. 263),
- direction setting (p. 179),
- energy management (p. 270),

- motivating (p.192) (self and others),
- imagination (p.247) (of the result),
- option generation (p.249),
- problem diagnosis (p.254),
- proactivity (p.281),
- self-awareness (p.285), and
- stress management (p.289).

E-MAIL MANAGEMENT

E-mails are taking up an increasing amount of our working lives. The pros of e-mails are that:

- they cut down on paper,
- they can be easily copied around the relevant people, and
- they can cut out the need for meetings.

The cons of e-mails are:

- they are often copied to people indiscriminately,
- they often lead to relatively little value creation per se (e.g. specific decisions or actions), but involve spreading information almost for its own sake, and
- they necessitate managers keeping up with their e-mail, which is both stressful and also may distract them from real work.

E-mails are thus very much a two-edged sword. It is not unknown for managers to receive anything between fifty and a hundred e-mails per day. (Ten years ago did you get fifty to a hundred letters per day? We don't think so!)

Deleting them is the most obvious trick. More proactive is to send an e-mail back to all senders who have sent you an e-mail relatively indiscriminately – in order for them to stop doing so in future. Although this requires some time investment, it can be worthwhile. (This is the same principle as weeding out junk mail.)

If you are going on holiday, e-mail those who have sent you e-mails in the last month/those who you might expect e-mails from, telling them you will be away (so don't send any non-important/urgent e-mails at all, or telling them when you can respond by. This means that your first day back is not going to be e-stressed.

Another thing you can do is to avoid sending indiscriminate e-mails yourself. Be clear what value you hope the e-mail will add: what do you want recipients to actually *do* with it?

Better still, agree an e-mail policy in your organization, with some dos and don'ts of e-mails.

A killer takeaway is as follows:

- Specify a more standard format for e-mails like:
  - Subject.
  - Key issues.
  - Options.
  - Value added.
  - Action needed.
  - Timings.
  - Who involved.

Obviously, where you cannot easily complete these headings, the sender should query whether the e-mail is worth sending in the first place!

E-mail management is thus very closely related to:

- option generation (p. 249),
- prioritization (p. 277),
- report writing (p. 227),
- stakeholder management (p. 199)
- time management (p. 291), and
- value management (p. 165).

ENERGY MANAGEMENT

nergy management entails being more aware of your energy levels, and being able to manage these – and even being able to increase your energy levels.

The pros of energy management are that it:

- avoids you getting too tired, so that you are no longer working effectively,
- avoids you becoming more prone to anxiety, frustration and irritability, and
- minimizes the risk of you getting ill.

We have already covered some of these issues in the section 'Energizing' (p. 184). One killer takeaway on energy management is to build your energy levels outside work, for example through going to the gym, yoga, and alternative treatments/activities like shiatsu (an energy-releasing massage).

Energy management links to:

- drive (p. 266),
- energizing (p. 184),
- motivating (p. 192), and
- self-awareness (p. 285).

LEARNING

L earning can be defined as: 'The feedback mechanism through which an individual (or a team) encounters and acts upon his/her environment, experiences the results of this activity as success or failure, and thus improves performance.'

The really outstanding manager is also an exceptional learner; in other words not only does he/she learn well, but this process is constantly pursued at a conscious and deliberate level.

The pros of learning are that it:

- creates a virtuous cycle of increasing performance through doing more of the right things/doing things better, and through avoiding errors, and
- creates a sense of achievement, of confidence, and thus a greater propensity to take measured risks.

One of the cons of learning is that it can make a manager unduly risk-averse: if something has not worked out in the past, it can result in an aversion to try it out again – either differently or in a different set of circumstances.

Learning can vary considerably in its complexity. It can be quite simple in nature, focusing on instrumental improvement of what you are already doing – sometimes called single-loop learning (Argyris 1991). Or, it can involve doing something in a very new way, or doing something quite differently – or double-loop learning (Argyris 1991). Finally it can involve exploring entirely new ways of dealing with a problem or issue – or strategic learning (Grundy 1994).

Some tools which are helpful for learning include:

- Fishbone analysis: see the section on problem diagnosis – why did something go wrong?
- Wishbone analysis: see the section on product development – why did something go right, and how?

- Forcefield analysis: see the section on change management – why was something difficult?
- Performance drivers: see 'Performance Analysis, p. 94 – why was performance good/bad?
- Uncertainty/importance grid: see 'Risk and Uncertainty Analysis', p. 44 – why did something go wrong?
- Stakeholder analysis: see 'Stakeholder Management' p. 199 – why did stakeholders support/not support something?

Killer takeaways on learning include:

- Before you tackle anything of any degree of complexity, ask yourself what has worked well/not so well elsewhere/in the past, and how can these lessons be tailored to the present situation?
- Tell stories (scenarios) about the future world – in which something works/doesn't work, and continuously monitor the situation for weak signals indicating that you are about to go into the world where things do not work out well.
- Detach yourself from any sense of personal regret and guilt. When extracting the learning lessons from a situation be as emotionally neutral as possible.

Learning is linked to:

- acquisition integration (p. 107),
- all strategy and marketing skills (p. 13ff and p. 53ff),
- benchmarking (p. 111),
- change management (p. 173),
- controlling (p. 116),
- creativity (p. 245),
- forecasting (p. 156),
- listening (p. 190),
- performance appraisal (p. 222),
- problem diagnosis (p. 254),
- questioning (p. 258),
- self-awareness (p. 285),
- self-development (p. 286),
- stakeholder management (p. 199),
- time management (p. 291), and
- turnaround (p. 158).

Reference

Argyris, C., 1991, 'Teaching Smart People How To Learn', *Harvard Business Review*, May–June 1991, pp 99–109.

Grundy, A.N. (1994) *Strategic Learning in Action*, McGraw Hill, Maidenhead.

PRESENTATIONS (MAKING THEM)

P resentations are a useful way of conveying information, diagnosis, options, proposals and their assumptions. Traditional presentations often suffer from a number of limitations because they often contain too much content, less interpretation, and are relatively one-way. Presentations should be seen as interactive vehicles for debate, rather than merely primarily as one-way communication devices.

Presentations can also be done instead in a far more summarized form, and one which we call 'the weather forecast' approach. Weather forecasters are quite different from normal presenters in so far as they:

- Do a very quick, high-level summary at the very beginning (for example, 'Tomorrow will be windy, wild, and wet').
- They then use visual representations of the weather, rather than rely purely or primarily on detailed bullet points.
- They do not cover *all* of the detail.
- They draw out the implications – the 'so what's?' as they go (such as 'on Friday we will see treacherous driving conditions').
- They present it – as far as is possible – as a storyline with linkages between issues.
- They quickly summarize it at the end, putting it in the wider/longer term context (for instance, 'after Wednesday, the weather will get a lot milder just in readiness for the Easter weekend').

In order to do this form of weather forecast presentation you will need to be able to:

- summarize well,
- draw out implications,
- determine in advance the points which you will either focus on, or leave out, or both, and

- use some pictorial methods (like SWOT, growth drivers, Porter's five competitive forces, or the strategic option grid etc.).

Another helpful tip is to leave pauses for some discussion. This is so that the recipients are able to comment briefly and ask questions as you go through the material, rather then having to suffer intellectual indigestion as more and more data is presented.

The strategic option grid is an ideal vehicle for this task as you can choose to concentrate more on some options or boxes within the grid, and less on others. You can also start at any point on the grid, rather than working through it in a very linear and predictable way.

One of the biggest things to avoid in presentations is being content-driven. This tendency is aggravated further by Microsoft PowerPoint, which encourages managers to over-elaborate content. Indeed one of the authors was shown a PowerPoint presentation on a company's strategic review. It contained nearly 200 slides, which must have cost a fortune and there was negligible discussion of strategic options and their implications! A more constructive approach is to punctuate the presentation with key discussion questions, or questions (unanswered) coming out of the material.

Listening to a presentation is another key skill, too. This involves:

- establishing the basis of judgements,
- identifying what *has not* been covered, and not just critiquing what has,
- questioning assumptions,
- identifying other options (not considered in the presentation),
- building a more cunning plan from it,
- identifying any inconsistencies within it, and
- asking yourself the question 'what is the one big thing which I have missed?'

Killer takeaways include:

- 'Props' can help you immeasurably – for example, bring along some samples of competitors' products, if looking at competitive position.
- Use (but do not overuse) humour, to liven it up – especially in conjunction with surprise.
- Develop a personal style, rather than just following convention.
- Don't go on for more than 10 to 15 minutes without punctuation – even if your input is absolutely fantastic!

Making presentations is linked to:

- business cases (p. 79),
- business planning (p. 82),
- direction setting (p. 179),
- influencing (p. 211),
- report writing (p. 227),
- questioning (p. 258),
- stakeholder management (p. 199), and
- summarizing (p. 202).

PRIORITIZATION

rioritization can be defined as: 'The process of resource allocation to establish which activities and projects should get most/
least resource, and over what timescales.'
    Prioritization is crucial because without it every activity gets
equal attention. As Sun Tzu once said:

> 'So when the front is prepared, the rear is lacking, and when
> the rear is prepared, the front is lacking. Preparedness on the
> left means lack on the right, preparedness on the right means
> lack on the left. But preparedness everywhere means lack every-
> where.'
> Sun Tzu, *The Art of War*

Or as Dilbert said:

> 'Having a strategy is about knowing when to say "No".'

Prioritization's advantages are that:

- it gives greater focus of resource allocation,
- it is more likely to lead to great competitive advantage – through the
  cunning plan,
- it helps simplify what needs to be communicated through the organization, and
- it increases flexibility and speed of movement/implementation.

Its potential disadvantages are that:

- prioritization can be hijacked for political and/or personal ends,
- lack of 'buy-in' to decisions may mean that there is dilution of
  organizational energy, and

- resources are still spread too thinly, as there is no decision not to do things up to do some of them later.

In the philosophy of breakthroughs (Grundy & Brown 2002), or *hoshin*, one is taught to undertake *no more than three* breakthrough projects within a particular time period. After achieving these, one can move on to other areas. For instance, breakthroughs for Tesco's in the late 1990s were: international strategic diversification, diversification into non-food, and reformatting its stores in the UK.

Several visual prioritization techniques exist (such as the strategic option grid – for more complex prioritization). In addition, attractiveness/implementation difficulty (AID) analysis can be used at a more micro level, as we shall now see (Fig. 10.1).

With AID analysis we begin with the vertical dimension of attractiveness one can now expand on the final bullet point above.

Only uncertainty (in the strategic option grid) is left out of the AID grid – so we have in AID analysis a much simpler prioritization technique, but one which does, however, omit uncertainty.

The strategic option grid and AID analysis are not mutually exclusive. The option grid can be used first to evaluate different strategic options (either for different projects, or for different ways of implement-

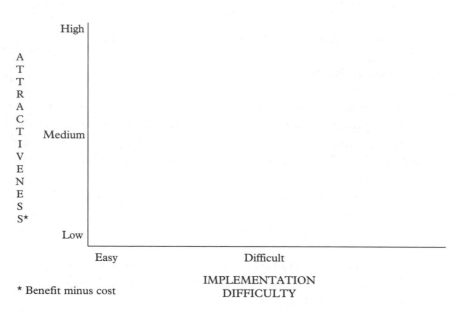

Fig. 10.1 Attractiveness/implementation difficulty analysis

ing a specific strategy). Then the AID analysis might evaluate and prioritize sub-parts of a specific option.

Sometimes parts of a possible strategy can be undertaken without doing others. For example, buying a business is a project but the constituent parts of the business can be regarded as sub-projects to be retained or possibly disposed of.

Even where a strategy does consist of a number of discretionary sub-parts, which are not discretionary (such as a training strategy), it is still possible to display their individual positionings on the AID grid. Without doubt some parts of the training will be more difficult to implement than others, and will thus have different positionings horizontally on the AID grid.

The AID grid enables trade-offs to be achieved between strategies. The vertical dimension of the picture focuses on benefits less costs. The horizontal dimension represents the total difficulty over time. This is the time up until delivery of results, and not of completion of earlier project phases. This tool therefore enables a portfolio of possible projects to be prioritized. Figure 10.2 illustrates a hypothetical case.

To summarize, AID analysis can be used:

- to prioritize strategic breakthroughs as a portfolio,
- to evaluate business plans, and

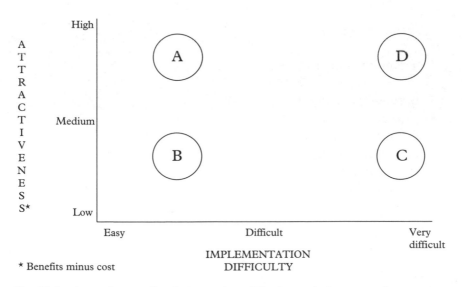

Fig. 10.1 Attractiveness/implementation difficulty analysis – example

- to evaluate the sub-components of a strategic breakthrough or project.

Its key benefits are that it is:

- a quick and easy technique to use, and
- a visual way of representing and debating priorities.

Its potential disadvantages are that:

- it can be subjective unless it is accompanied by further analysis – for example, analysis of value and cost drivers for attractiveness or of forcefield analysis implementation difficulty (see 'Change Management', p. 173), and
- it can just represent existing thinking on a breakthrough rather than, more creatively, the cunning plan.

Killer takeaways on prioritization include:

- Instead of focusing on identifying highest priority items, identify the least, and then drop these off.
- Don't finalize your prioritization without first considering the cunning plan for any projects which are just below the 'go' decision threshold, and also without doing storytelling of those just above the 'go' threshold.

Prioritization links to:

- action planning (p. 263),
- cost management (p. 146),
- business planning (p. 82),
- project appraisal (p. 98),
- resource management (p. 131),
- targeting goals (p. 100),
- time management (p. 291), and
- turnaround (p. 158).

PROACTIVITY

roactivity can be defined as being: 'Those behaviours and mind-sets which are targeted at creating the future, rather than dealing with the consequences of the past.'

To illustrate that there is a continuum between reactive and proactivity consider the statement that 'the world of managers can be divided into:

- those who are unaware of what is happening to them, and/or why,
- those who are aware of it, but who just watch it happening,
- those who are aware of what might happen in the future, but don't know how they might deal with it, and
- those who create their own futures (obviously being the most proactive)'.

Proactivity has a number of key advantages for the average manager:

- you are far more likely to succeed, for example in difficult talks like project management – and in less time, with less difficulty, and with less resource,
- you will be far less stressed out,
- you will be able to work shorter hours, and
- your readiness for promotion should be accelerated.

Whilst there are no easy fixes for how to become more proactive, there are a large number of clues in this book which should be of great help. These include:

- Wishbone analysis (see 'Product Development', p. 69), for defining what you 'really-really-really want,' and for helping you to establish the alignment conditions which will deliver this.

- The uncertainty/importance grid (see 'Risk and Uncertainty Analysis', p. 44), for identifying the major downsides which might impact on these alignment factors.
- Storytelling the future.
- Fishbone analysis – for anticipating the future events that will lead to problems.

In addition, we can also use a further technique for proactivity called the importance/influence grid (see Fig. 10.3). Here importance and influence analysis helps us to look at the extent to which we *do* have control over various strategic factors, or we *do not* have control.

Attention is often drawn more to those areas which we have *most* influence over – and which are considered to be most important – rather than those which are *both* most important, *and* where we have least influence (the southeast zone of the importance/influence grid).

Yet it is frequently possible – through creative thinking – to get at least some influence over these areas of apparent low influence.

Importance/influence analysis can be used:

- as part of a scenario development process,
- when influencing stakeholders: to determine where the key points of their vulnerability influence might be, and

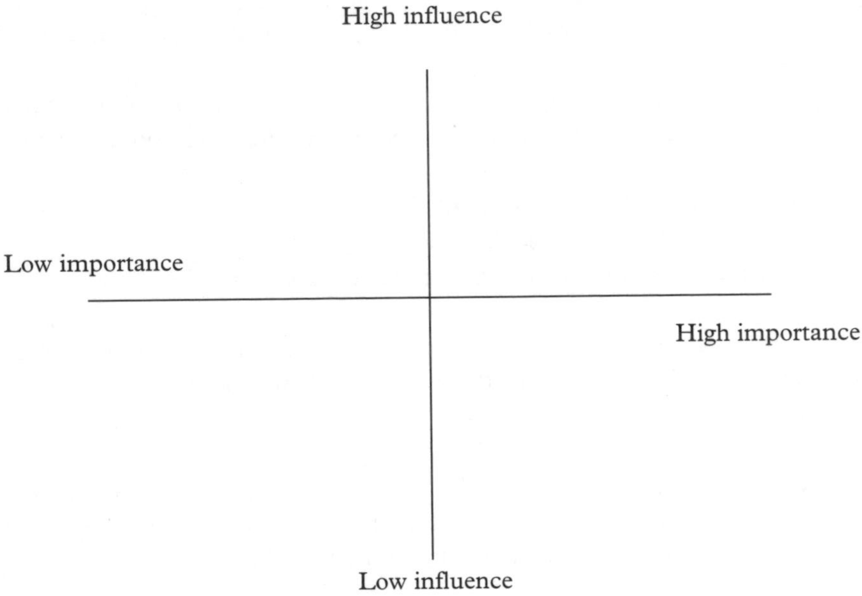

Fig. 10.3   Importance/influence grid

- to challenge one's own mindset – that some things are simply beyond one's control.

The key benefits of importance/influence analysis are that it:

- forces managers to think more proactively about what they can do about issues, and
- helps them scan their own external and internal environment – and acts as a focus for action.

Finally, in order to scan immediate priorities (as a way of becoming more proactive), the urgency/importance grid (originally created by Stephen Covey) is very helpful (see Fig. 10.4).

This urgency/importance grid is typically used to position Post-it® notes symbolizing each issue or project. With this grid it is important however to avoid overfocusing on the most urgent at the expense of the most important.

The urgency/importance grid can also help you in time management. For example, spend 80 per cent of your time on the few, really important projects, focusing on them all at once. Then spend the remaining 20 per cent of your time (on dedicated days or half-days) to specialize in clearing the less important projects before they become too urgent and distracting.

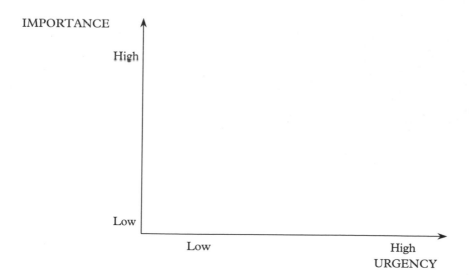

Fig. 10.4 Urgency/importance grid

Killer takeaways on proactivity are:

- Imagine you are actually in the future (of a particular time and in a particular situation).
- If there is a threat or problem, then consider – how can you turn this threat into an opportunity?
- Where something appears to be very difficult, what are the things which are already inherent in the situation which you could use to make it easier?
- If someone seems to be both influential and against a particular proposal, ask them what turns them off most about it. Also what might turn them on? Also, can they see some other option for achieving the proposal's goals?

Proactivity has links to:

SELF-AWARENESS

Self-awareness is a difficult skill to develop as, inevitably, you are inclined to focus on what is happening around you, rather than in trying to observe your own behaviour. Self-awareness is helpful because it will allow you to deal with issues with more objectivity. Being *too* aware of oneself can, however, result in a decline in self-confidence.

There are a number of techniques for enhancing self-awareness (as covered elsewhere in this book). These include:

- The out-of-body experience – for trying to see how others see you, or for trying to take an external perspective outside your behaviour.
- Fishbone analysis – for understanding what *you* might be doing to cause an interpersonal problem, or conflict.
- Stakeholder analysis – to gain a better understanding of what is on your own agendas – and thus your underlying drivers.

In addition, there is a range of psychometric techniques which can help you to understand your personal styles, including:

- Belbin (for your default team role), and
- OPQ or Myers Briggs or Erickson-McCann tests – for your personality types (like extrovert/introvert, intuitive versus thinking etc.).

Some killer takeaways on self-awareness include:

- Think back to these incidents in the past where you have overachieved/underachieved. Why did these instances happen, and what do these reveal about your strengths and weaknesses?
- Which meetings do people invite you to, and what kind of role do they expect you to play most – because you seem to be good at it?

Self-awareness invariably links closely to self-development, as we see next.

SELF-DEVELOPMENT

S elf-development is the process of taking full ownership over the way in which one develops one's own skills and career, both strategically and tactically. Self-development has a number of key benefits:

- you do not wait for others to come along and develop you, nor to provide you with career opportunities, and
- you are able to have more control over your career, including possible moves laterally and vertically within your organization – and outside it, too.

Self-development includes:

- identifying your current skills and your strengths and weaknesses,
- defining the gap between your current skills base and your present role requirements,
- defining where you want to be at some future stage of your career,
- developing a number of potential career strategies to achieve your career goals, and
- defining the skills gap between where you are now and want to be, given your above thoughts.

These skills breakthroughs and areas of continuous improvement can then be prioritized using either AID analysis, or the urgency/importance grid (see Fig. 10.4, p. 283).

Management development is seen very much as a central vehicle of self-development. In particular, doing an MBA can be a useful way of accelerating your self-development. The advantages of doing an MBA (Grundy & Brown 2003) are:

- it gives you a broader skill-set,

- it should help you to develop your helicopter thinking, and global awareness,
- it will give you greater self-confidence,
- it should develop your interpersonal skills,
- it might broaden your career opportunities, both in and outside your function and organization, and even outside your industry, and
- it ought to increase your pay, and give you greater long-term security – through flexibility.

The cons of doing an MBA are:

- it can be expensive,
- it may not necessarily advance your career much, if you do not actually get a more challenging role afterwards,
- it may not do an awful lot for your career if the course is not at a particularly well-known institution, and
- if you do a full-time MBA, and if the executive job market slumps, you might find it difficult and time consuming to get a job again following the completion of the MBA – especially at your desired, premium salary level.

Having said that, an MBA is a long-term, strategic decision, so tactical factors need to be weighed carefully against the strategic benefits.

Killer takeaways on self-development include:

- Imagine yourself in a future role, say five, or even ten years into the future – how did you develop yourself in order to get there?
- Don't even think about an MBA unless you have defined your career objectives, strategy and other developmental options first.

Self-development links to:

- action planning (p. 263),
- coaching (p. 177),
- drive (p. 266),
- learning (p. 271),
- performance appraisal (p. 222),
- self-awareness (p. 285),
- time management (p. 291), and
- training (p. 232).

References

Grundy, A.N. & Brown, L., (2003) *Developing the Individual,* Capstone Publishing, Oxford.

STRESS MANAGEMENT

tress can be defined as: 'The general unpleasant experience of feeling that the demands on you exceed your capacity to deal with them. Stress management is now defined as being the process of managing stress, both proactively and through coping strategies, in order to avoid it, or to minimize its impact.'

Surprisingly, organizational theorists debate a lot with each other as to whether stress even exists. (Possibly these theorists are mainly debating whether the word 'stress' is a meaningful category which helps us to explain things.)

Indeed *it is* true that stress denotes not only a large variety of symptoms (for example, anxiety, depression, tiredness, irritation, frustration and anger), but also causes. Causes of stress might include uncertainty, role tension and ambiguity, role overload, conflict, and anxiety about your job security or possibilities for future career advancement etc. But the truth is that stress is a very meaningful word to most managers as it sums up how they are feeling a lot of the time. So how can it be managed? If we look first at managing its causes (rather than its symptoms) it may be helpful – both from an organizational and individual perspective:

- To ensure that organizational communication is as clear and as open as possible, to minimize unnecessary uncertainty and ambiguity.
- For the individual – to own their own career (and the self-development), and to continuously review and update their career options – so that they don't feel irrevocably trapped in a specific career role.
- To do scenario storytelling about the future environment (both internal and external) of the organization – thus minimizing any bad surprises – and also to give some lead-time to take evasive action pending disruptive change.
- To understand the causes of your stress. For example, using fishbone analysis, data can be used to discuss how unnecessary causes of

stress can be alleviated, either during your appraisal, or in an ongoing way with your boss.

- Through improved energy management and time management (see p. 270 and p. 291).
- Through avoiding working longer hours to keep up with job demands. If you are having to do this then you have either got an unfair workload, or you are being efficient but not fully effective (i.e. not doing all of the right things). Or, you are in a vicious cycle of getting more and more tired – making you less and less efficient.
- Through better delegation/prioritization, or through re-engineering of your role.

As an illustration on this last point: if you work a ten hour day for a long time you are probably going to be about 85% efficient relative to an eight hour day. So you are only gaining an apparent equivalent of half an hour's productivity. But if you fall ill for five days as a result of overwork then this would dissipate away a further half your extra productivity!

Killer takeaways on stress management are:

- Use gap analysis, together with project managing your job, to know in advance what your available capacity is over the next days/weeks/months. This will enable you to say whether – and when – you can take on further work. You will also be able to flag up which other activities will now be either delayed, diluted, or not done at all.
- Be prepared to say 'no', albeit in a polite way, by saying for example: 'I don't think I will really be able to do this and get the result that we need in that timescale – unless you/we can think of options of how I could get it done in a really cunning way.'

Stress management thus has clear links to:

- creativity (p. 245),
- delegation (p. 209),
- energy management (p. 270),
- influencing (p. 211),
- motivating (p. 192),
- prioritization (p. 277),
- proactivity (p. 281),
- stakeholder management (p. 199), and
- time management (p. 291).

TIME MANAGEMENT

 ime management is a very important skill for managers at all levels. Time management can turn you into an extremely effective manager. Not only can it allow you to eat your way through a much bigger workload, but it can also help you get a better balance of life, and conserve your energy.

Time management techniques include:

- prioritization techniques (strategic option grid), AID analysis, urgency/importance grids,
- fishbone analysis if you find yourself asking the question, 'why do I find it hard to manage my time effectively?', and
- plotting the value-over-time curve (see Fig 10.5). This allows you to target and monitor the value over time of your activities – for example of your day, of a project, or of a particular meeting.

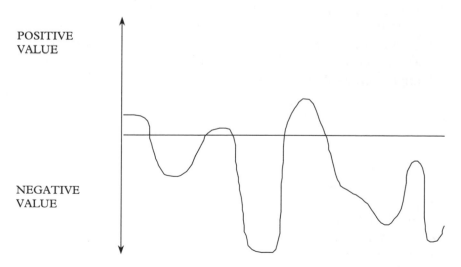

Fig. 10.5 The value-over-time curve

As an illustration of the potential for time-saving one sales director (responsible for 300 staff) used fishbone analysis to cut his average week down by 7 hours from about 67 hours to 60 hours. Since then (three years ago), he has saved approximately 1000 hours! (This 7 hours a week was spent in 'nice-to-dos' – both meetings and in reading industry reports.) One thing that he needed to do to achieve this breakthrough was to start to say no (gently) to attending meetings where his value was going to be relatively peripheral, and mainly symbolic in nature.

Truly effective time management therefore requires significant re-engineering of one's role. For example, one of the authors used to spend about 25 per cent of his time as a consultant in marketing and selling activities. Much of this time was relatively unproductive – it was spent in telephoning potential clients (who were often not available at the time he called), and on speculative meetings.

Instead, by writing a number of publications, by becoming a lecturer at a business school, and by building a better network of contacts he found that this unproductive time fell from 25 to 5 per cent – resulting in a major increase in leisure time and profitability.

Killer takeaways in time management now include:

- Think how you can do an activity in half the time, or even less.
- Think about how you can get twice the value out of an activity.
- Use a mental colour code for your attendance at meetings/other activities:
  - green: I am adding significant value,
  - yellow: I am adding moderate value, and
  - red: I am either not adding real value at all, or I am actually destroying value.
- Split your role into a number of projects, then ask 'if I were to start again from scratch, which ones would I actually do?', and stop or migrate out of the rest.

Time management links to:

- delegation (p. 209),
- direction setting (p. 179),
- helicopter thinking (p. 40),
- prioritization (p. 277),
- problem diagnosis (p. 254),
- self-awareness (p. 285), and
- self-development (p. 286),
- value management (p. 165).

Some Case Studies Linked to the 100 Business Skills

The Body Shop

A case study of The Body Shop can be found in *Exploring Strategic Financial Management* (Grundy 1998). The case study is mainly financial, but contains some links to strategy marketing and organization. It covers the period to around 1996.

Skills illustrated include:

- brand management,
- customer awareness,
- direction setting,
- option generation,
- organizational design,
- strategic thinking,
- storytelling,
- understanding company accounts, and
- value management.

BMW/Rover

BMW/Rover is a strategy and acquisition case that looks at acquisition options, valuations, integration and learning. A case study can be found in Grundy (2003) *Acquisitions and Mergers*. A longer study is to be found in a dedicated book by Chris Brady and Andrew Lorenz called *BMW and Rover – a Brand Too Far* (2001).

Specific skills that are included are as follows:

- acquisitions and deal-making,
- acquisitions appraisal,
- acquisition integration,

- alliances,
- brand awareness,
- change management,
- competitor awareness,
- cost management,
- customer awareness,
- direction setting,
- economic awareness (micro),
- financial planning,
- global awareness,
- margin management,
- negotiation,
- option generation,
- organizational design,
- prioritization,
- product development,
- risk and uncertainty analysis,
- storytelling,
- strategic thinking,
- turnaround, and
- value management.

Champneys

Champneys is an example of a turnaround case, where an upmarket leisure group needed to rediscover its competitive advantage. A study, which examines strategy, marketing, finance, operations, organization and leadership can be found in *Be Your Own Strategy Consultant* (Grundy & Brown 2002) – strategy version – or in *Strategic Project Management* (Grundy & Brown 2002) – project management version – or in *Value-Based HR Strategy* (Grundy & Brown 2003) – HR strategy version.

Specific skills in the case include:

- brand management,
- change management,
- cost management,
- customer awareness
- direction setting,
- economic awareness,
- empathizing,
- energizing,

- global awareness,
- life-cycle management,
- listening,
- market development,
- organization design,
- performance analysis,
- prioritization,
- problem-solving,
- product development,
- project management,
- stakeholder management,
- teamworking
- turnaround, and
- value management.

British Telecom

A case study in *Strategic Behaviour* (Grundy 1998) examines the case of BT over several chapters, focusing on how teams behave when evolving strategy. There are obviously links to strategy skills.

Skills illustrated include:

- brainstorming,
- chairing,
- challenging,
- helicopter thinking,
- presentations,
- prioritization,
- problem diagnosis,
- summarizing,
- teamworking, and
- time management.

Dowty Case Communications and Mercury Communications cases

Dowty Case Communications and Mercury Communications case studies which integrate strategy and many of the organizational skills, including learning. They show how a strategy can be used as a learning process – and the pitfalls. Both cases are to be found in *Developing the Individual* (Grundy & Brown 2003).

Key skills include:

- business planning,
- learning,
- organization and people planning,
- process management,
- project management,
- strategic thinking, and
- training.

Dyson

The Dyson case study is about the evolution of a growth company through a fast-maturing life cycle, and one where brand, innovation and organizational flexibility play a key role. It is found in *Smart Things to Know about Growth* (Grundy 2003) and in *Be Your Own Strategy Consultant* (Grundy & Brown 2002).

Specific skills in the case include:

- brand management,
- cash-flow management,
- chairing,
- competitor awareness,
- creativity,
- customer awareness,
- energizing,
- financial planning,
- global awareness,
- margin management,
- market development,
- organizational design,
- product development,
- storytelling,
- strategic thinking, and
- turnaround.

HP

HP is a short case study in *Be Your Own Strategy Consultant* (Grundy & Brown 2002) on mentoring and its impact on strategic thinking of a senior manager at HP.

Key skills illustrated include:

- coaching,
- direction setting,
- helicopter thinking,
- learning,
- prioritization,
- problem diagnosis,
- self-awareness,
- stakeholder management, and
- time management.

Manchester United and Arsenal cases

The Manchester United case integrates financial and strategic skills. The Arsenal case looks at how a business can be managed as a bundle of projects, and also at the softer, organizational determinants of business performance. The Manchester United case is in *Exploring Strategic Financial Management* (Grundy 1998) and the Arsenal case study in *Strategic Project Management* (Grundy & Brown 2002).

Key skills include:

- acquisitions (of players),
- brand management,
- divestment (of players),
- option generation,
- organization and people planning,
- project appraisal,
- project management,
- strategic thinking,
- storytelling, and
- understanding company accounts.

Marks & Spencer

Marks & Spencer is a classic case study integrating strategy, marketing, finance, and organization change and leadership. It explores M&S's evolution through the 1990s to the present time and the options that it might have considered *Be Your Own Strategy Consultant* (Grundy & Brown 2002). Judi Bevans' book *The Rise and Fall of Marks & Spencer* (2001) is a full study of M&S – and one which is hard to put down.

Key skills include:

- brand management,
- chairing,
- change management,
- competitor awareness,
- cost management,
- customer awareness,
- economic awareness,
- global awareness,
- option generation,
- political awareness,
- prioritization,
- recruitment,
- storytelling,
- strategic thinking,
- turnaround,
- understanding company accounts, and
- value management.

The Prudential

In *Strategic Project Management* (Grundy & Brown 2002), a study of the Prudential examines the issues around project managing change – and the leadership issues which this implies.

Key skills covered include:

- change management
- direction setting,
- facilitation,
- learning,
- project management,

- organization and people planning,
- performance analysis, and
- teamworking.

Conclusion

T here may well be at least a hundred key business skills for you to master, as we have tried to show in this book. But the real art is to draw from these on a just-in-time basis, a unique set for each situation – and to become adept as a genuinely superior manager.

Our book ought at least to have made you more aware of both when and how you are exercising these skills, as well as what your most important skills gaps are. In writing this book we have drawn from our own tacit skills developed in a multitude of industries and roles, besides the more formal skills picked up through doing MBAs, and through studying the diverse skills of business management.

We also hope that you will look beyond the various visually based management skills – in the form of numerous figures representing management tools and techniques – and that you will actively experiment with these. Using them has transformed the way in which we, and others, have managed the many dilemmas and ambiguities in business, and have helped to bring a particular freshness and incisiveness to the task of managing.

You – as our reader – might well find it opportune to revisit your original diagnostic scores on these skills, perhaps three or six months after your original reading of the book – to see how these have evolved. Our intention is to have all these messages to yourselves working at least at a sub-conscious level and hopefully a lot more.

And perhaps our anecdotes have given you a sense that management is, at its best, more of the nature of being 'skilful play' than some kind of advanced business science. Fortunately, there are *no more* than one hundred key business skills, but the permutations of these skills are practically endless.

Most managers enjoy (generally) superior incomes but perhaps there are other pay-offs, too. But just maybe, the idea of business skills as 'skilful play' will not only make your business skills more fluid and innovative, but will also diminish the stress and (perceived) drudgery which many managers experience on a day-to-day basis.

Best of luck!

Dr Tony Grundy and Dr Laura Brown

References

Ansoff, I. (1969) *Corporate Strategy*, Irwin, Homewood.

Argyris, C., 'Teaching Smart People How to Learn', *Harvard Business Review*, pp 99–109, May–June 1991.

Bartlett, C. and Ghoshal, S. (1989) *Managing Across Borders*, Harvard Business School Press, MA.

Bennett, Stewart G. III. (1991) *The Quest for Value – The EVA Management Guide*, HarperBusiness, NY.

Bevan, J. (2001) *The Rise and Fall of Marks & Spencer*, Profile Books, London.

Brady, C. & Lorenz, A. (2001) *BMW and Rover – A Brand Too Far*, FT Publishing, London.

Burch, G. (1994) *Resistance is Useless*, Capstone Press, Oxford.

Doyle, P. (1994) *Marketing Management and Strategy*, Prentice Hall, Hemel Hempstead.

Faulkner, D. (1995) *International Alliances*, McGraw Hill, Maidenhead.

Grant, R.M. 'The Resource-Based Theory of Competitive Advantage: Implications for Strategy Formulation', *California Management Review*, Spring 1991, pp. 114–135.

Grundy, A.N. (1994) *Strategic Learning in Action*, McGraw Hill, Maidenhead.

Grundy, A.N. (1998) *Exploring Strategic Financial Management*, Prentice Hall, Hemel Hempstead – especially the chapter on 'Strategic Financial Accounting'.

Grundy, A.N. (1998) *Strategic Behaviour*, FT Publishing, London.

Grundy, A.N. & Brown, L. (2002a) *Strategic Project Management*, Thomson Publishing, London.

Grundy, A.N. & Brown, L. (2002b) *Be Your Own Strategy Consultant*, Thomson Publishing, London.

Grundy, A.N. (2002) *Shareholder Value*, Capstone Press, Oxford.

Grundy, A.N. (2003) *Smart Things to Know About Acquisitions and Mergers*, Capstone Publishing, Oxford.

Grundy, A.N. & Brown, L. (2003a) *Developing the Individual,* Capstone Press, Oxford.

Grundy, A.N. & Brown, L. (2003b) *Value-Based HR Strategy,* Butterworth-Heinemann, Oxford.

Hamel, G. and Prahalad, C.K. (1994) *Competing for the Future,* Harvard Business School Press, MA.

Hammer, G. and Champy, J. (1993) *Re-engineering the Corporation,* Nicholas Brealy Publishing, London.

Haspeslagh, P.C. and Jemison, D.B. (1991) *Managing Acquisitions,* The Free Press/Macmillan, NY.

Kaplan, R.S. & Norton, D.P. 'The Balanced Scorecard – Measures that Drive Performance', *Harvard Business Review,* January–February, 1992.

Kotler, P. (1984) *Marketing Management,* Englewood Cliffs, NJ.

Mintzberg, H. (1994) *The Rise and Fall of Strategic Planning,* Prentice Hall, Hemel Hempstead.

Mitroff, I.I., & Linstone, H.A. (1993) *The Unbounded Mind,* Oxford University Press, Oxford.

Porter, E.M. (1980) *Competitive Strategy,* The Free Press, Macmillan, NY.

Porter, E.M. (1985) *Competitive Advantage,* The Free Press, Macmillan, NY.

Senge, P. (1990) *The Fifth Discipline: The Art & Practice of the Learning Organization,* Doubleday, NJ.

Yip, G. (1992) *Total Global Strategy,* Prentice Hall, Englewood Cliffs, NJ.

INDEX